D0728271

Cancer

Other Books of Related Interest:

Opposing Viewpoints Series

Alternative Medicine

Medicine

Current Controversies

Cancer

Health Care

At Issue Series

Pandemics

Sexually Transmitted Diseases

CONTEMPORARY
ISSUES
COMPANION

Cancer

Clayton Farris Naff, Book Editor

GREENHAVEN PRESS
A part of Gale, Cengage Learning

GALE
CENGAGE Learning

Detroit • New York • San Francisco • New Haven, Conn • Waterville, Maine • London

GALE
CENGAGE Learning·

Christine Nasso, *Publisher*
Elizabeth Des Chenes, *Managing Editor*

© 2008 Greenhaven Press, a part of Gale, Cengage Learning.

For more information, contact:
Greenhaven Press
27500 Drake Rd.
Farmington Hills, MI 48331-3535
Or you can visit our Internet site at gale.cengage.com

Articles in Greenhaven Press anthologies are often edited for length to meet page require-ments. In addition, original titles of these works are changed to clearly present the main thesis and to explicitly indicate the author's opinion. Every effort is made to ensure that Greenhaven Press accurately reflects the original intent of the authors. Every effort has been made to trace the owners of copyrighted material.

Cover photograph reproduced by permission of © Royalty-Free/Corbis.

LIBRARY OF CONGRESS CATALOGING-IN-PUBLICATION DATA

Cancer / Clayton Farris Naff, book editor.
p. cm. -- (Contemporary issues companion)
Includes bibliographical references and index.
ISBN-13: 978-0-7377-2444-8 (hardcover)
ISBN-10: 0-7377-2444-7 (hardcover)
ISBN-13: 978-0-7377-2445-5 (pbk.)
ISBN-10: 0-7377-2445-5 (pbk.)
1. Cancer--Juvenile literature I. Naff, Clay Farris.
RC264.C35 2008
616.99'4--dc22

2007035069

Printed in the United States of America
2 3 4 5 6   13 12 11 10 09
ED063

Contents

Foreword

In the news, on the streets, and in neighborhoods, individuals are confronted with a variety of social problems. Such problems may affect people directly: A young woman may struggle with depression, suspect a friend of having bulimia, or watch a loved one battle cancer. And even the issues that do not directly affect her private life—such as religious cults, domestic violence, or legalized gambling—still impact the larger society in which she lives. Discovering and analyzing the complexities of issues that encompass communal and societal realms as well as the world of personal experience is a valuable educational goal in the modern world.

Effectively addressing social problems requires familiarity with a constantly changing stream of data. Becoming well informed about today's controversies is an intricate process that often involves reading myriad primary and secondary sources, analyzing political debates, weighing various experts' opinions—even listening to firsthand accounts of those directly affected by the issue. For students and general observers, this can be a daunting task because of the sheer volume of information available in books, periodicals, on the evening news, and on the Internet. Researching the consequences of legalized gambling, for example, might entail sifting through congressional testimony on gambling's societal effects, examining private studies on Indian gaming, perusing numerous Web sites devoted to Internet betting, and reading essays written by lottery winners as well as interviews with recovering compulsive gamblers. Obtaining valuable information can be time-consuming—since it often requires researchers to pore over numerous documents and commentaries before discovering a source relevant to their particular investigation.

Greenhaven's Contemporary Issues Companion series seeks to assist this process of research by providing readers with useful and pertinent information about today's complex issues. Each volume in this anthology series focuses on a topic of current interest, presenting informative and thought-provoking selections written from a wide variety of viewpoints. The readings selected by the editors include such diverse sources as personal accounts and case studies, pertinent factual and statistical articles, and relevant commentaries and overviews. This diversity of sources and views, found in every Contemporary Issues Companion, offers readers a broad perspective in one convenient volume.

In addition, each title in the Contemporary Issues Companion series is designed especially for young adults. The selections included in every volume are chosen for their accessibility and are expertly edited in consideration of both the reading and comprehension levels of the audience. The structure of the anthologies also enhances accessibility. An introductory essay places each issue in context and provides helpful facts such as historical background or current statistics and legislation that pertain to the topic. The chapters that follow organize the material and focus on specific aspects of the book's topic. Every essay is introduced by a brief summary of its main points and biographical information about the author. These summaries aid in comprehension and can also serve to direct readers to material of immediate interest and need. Finally, a comprehensive index allows readers to efficiently scan and locate content.

The Contemporary Issues Companion series is an ideal launching point for research on a particular topic. Each anthology in the series is composed of readings taken from an extensive gamut of resources, including periodicals, newspapers, books, government documents, the publications of private and public organizations, and Internet Web sites. In these volumes, readers will find factual support suitable for use in reports, debates, speeches, and research papers. The anthologies also facilitate further research, featuring a book and periodical bibliography and a list of organizations to contact for additional information.

A perfect resource for both students and the general reader, Greenhaven's Contemporary Issues Companion series is sure to be a valued source of current, readable information on social problems that interest young adults. It is the editors' hope that readers will find the Contemporary Issues Companion series useful as a starting point to formulate their own opinions about and answers to the complex issues of the present day.

Introduction

The war on cancer is America's longest-running conflict. President Richard Nixon declared the metaphorical war during his January 1971 State of the Union address. In his speech, he said: "The time has come in America when the same kind of concentrated effort that split the atom and took man to the moon should be turned toward conquering this dread disease. Let us make a total national commitment to achieve this goal." Congress followed with the National Cancer Act of 1971, and the war was on.

A quarter of a century later, oncologist John Bailar III raised the specter of defeat in an article published in the prestigious *New England Journal of Medicine*. By 2006, the thirty-fifth anniversary of the "war on cancer," whole books and numerous articles declaring failure were being published.

Indeed, there are reasons for the gloom. Cancer remains a leading cause of death, second only to heart disease in the United States. Every three minutes, two Americans die from cancer. According to the American Cancer Society, if current trends continue, cancer will be the leading cause of death in the United States by 2010. One in five Americans will die from cancer.

Statistics such as these lead many commentators to sense defeat. Writing in the *National Journal*, columnist Ned Rice declares, "It's time to face the fact that the war on cancer is over, and that cancer has won."

However, few researchers in the field would go that far. The general consensus is that the war indeed has yet to be won, but great progress has been made, and the goal of conquering cancer remains in sight.

Why Cancer Is So Hard to Treat

Cancer is not a foreign invader but a rebellion from within. The cartoon character Pogo famously said, "We have met the enemy, and he is us." That is a good description of cancer. Unlike contagious diseases, in which a bacterium or virus attacks the body, cancer is a disease in which the patient's own cells go haywire and begin to multiply wildly.

Cancer comes in more than a hundred varieties, all characterized by the abnormal, unending growth of an organism's own cells. Cancerous cells often develop into tumors (tissue masses) that can disrupt or destroy healthy organs.

Normal cells have a life cycle, just as organisms do. They grow, multiply, and die in an orderly fashion. In the developmental years of life, normal cells multiply in a rapid but controlled fashion to allow a child to grow into an adult. After that, cells in most parts of the body split to form new cells only when necessary to replace worn-out or dying cells or to heal an injury.

There is a reason for the restraint. Normal cells have a limit on the number of times they can divide. This limit is determined by a kind of cellular odometer called a telomere. Every time a cell divides, the telomere gets one unit shorter. When the last unit disappears, it triggers a process called apoptosis, or programmed cell death. Apoptosis is the main safety mechanism in a multicellular organism against the outbreak of cancer.

However, telomeres are located on the tips of chromosomes, which are the loops of DNA (deoxyribonucleic acid) at the heart of each cell. When the DNA in a given cell is damaged in a particular way, telomeres can no longer trigger apoptosis, and the cell begins to divide without purpose or limit. In short, cancer has taken hold.

DNA damage can result from a wide variety of causes. Highly energetic radiation, such as X-rays, can disrupt the molecular structure of DNA. So can viruses, which inject their own DNA into a cell. Carcinogenic (that is, cancer-causing) assaults on DNA include tobacco smoke, asbestos, and even excess fat.

Whatever the origin of cancer, the dilemma for treatment is the same. To kill cancer cells without harming normal cells is extremely difficult, because they all have the same DNA, and because after the initial outbreak, cancer cells may be found anywhere in the body. Any cancer cell in a tumor may break loose and float through the bloodstream to start a new tumor somewhere else.

Hope for the Future

Despite the difficulties, and the pessimism of some commentators, there is genuine hope for great strides in the management if not outright conquest of cancer. Three broad areas of progress stand out.

First, the public is learning how to reduce the risk of cancer. As a result, beginning in 2003 the number of cancer deaths in America began to show a slight but notable decline. That decline continued in 2004, and actually grew significantly. There were 3,014 fewer deaths from cancer that year. That is tiny compared with the estimated 560,000 annual cancer fatalities in America, but it is meaningful all the same.

The main reason for the drop is that fewer people are smoking, and those who continue to smoke are under growing restrictions. Exposure to tobacco smoke is the single greatest known risk factor for cancer. According to the American Cancer Society (ACS), about 40 percent of the decline in cancer rates among men is attributable to reduced smoking. The rate of smoking has dropped by half since the mid-1970s, saving millions of lives. However, the ACS warns that there are signs of a stall in the decline in smoking, which could jeopardize or even reverse the decline in cancer.

Cancer researchers also fear that the obesity epidemic sweeping the United States could put an end to the drop in cancer deaths. Obesity is a prominent risk factor for cancer. For these and other reasons, no one is ready to project a durable decline in cancer rates. John R. Seffrin, head of the

American Cancer Society, concludes that "we may be losing momentum in some key areas that have been critical to our success."

The second area of progress is in the detection and treatment of cancer. New diagnostic tools, such as improved medical imaging, have made it easier to catch cancer in its early stages. A prime example is computer-aided tomography, better known as the CAT scan. This technology engages a computer to combine numerous X-ray images into a single, highly detailed picture of the patient's interior. It has greatly aided the detection of cancer. So much so, indeed, that Dr. Michael Forsting, head of radiology at the University Clinic in Essen, Germany, calls computer tomography "the biggest quantum leap forward in medicine since the discovery of antibiotics."

Effective screening means early detection, and early detection is key to the successful treatment of most cancers.

A Growing Armory of Treatments

Since the inception of the "war on cancer," many promising treatments for cancer have ended in disappointment. Nevertheless, many significant improvements have been made in the two main branches of treatment: radiation and chemotherapy.

The first therapy kills tumor cells with high-energy radiation, such as X-rays. The danger is that healthy cells may also die. New techniques have improved targeting and deliver the beams from a variety of angles so as to minimize the exposure of healthy cells while repeatedly irradiating cancerous cells.

Chemotherapy aims to poison cancer cells without killing the patient. It is a delicate balance, one that often brings misery during the treatment. Chemotherapy often kills the follicle cells that produce hair and the cells lining the intestine. The result is temporary baldness, nausea, and indigestion. However, the rapid development of new cancer drugs has meant ever-more discriminating chemotherapy, with fewer side effects and a greater kill rate for cancer cells.

Additionally, improvements in adjuvant therapy—the continued administration of anticancer drugs to patients whose symptoms have disappeared—have greatly contributed to the long-term survival of those stricken with cancer.

Together, improvements in early detection and screening have made great inroads into the mortality rate of such major pathologies as breast cancer. Donald Berry, chair of the Department of Biostatistics and Applied Mathematics at the M.D. Anderson Cancer Center, says, "Screening would have no benefit if not followed by treatment, including surgery, and treatment has the potential to be more effective if cancer is detected at earlier stages by screening."

On the horizon are radical new strategies that may do even more to fight cancer. Angio-statins are drugs that act to block the formation of new blood vessels. Experiments show that they can choke off the supply of blood to tumors. Folate-immune treatment hopes to marshal the body's immune system by flagging tumor cells as hostile. These are just two examples from a host of possibilities that researchers are investigating.

The war against cancer has not been won, and indeed it may never be won. Cancer, after all, is a part of ourselves. Nevertheless, while we may not conquer cancer, there is every indication that we will learn to manage it.

CHAPTER 1

Cancer: Its Causes and Symptoms

Skin Cancer and Sunlight

Christopher McDougall

In the following selection writer Christopher McDougall reveals the growing threat of skin cancer to men. Increasingly, doctors are discovering the disease in men under forty, and in boys as young as twelve. One type is slow-growing and rarely fatal, but the other, melanoma, spreads rapidly and often kills.

Fortunately, skin cancer is easy to detect, because it starts on the surface of the body. All it takes is recognition by an individual that a mole or freckle is undergoing some sort of change. However, many people, men in particular, according to McDougall, are reluctant to acknowledge that what they see might be cancer, and even more reluctant to have it examined by a doctor. Early detection is key to successful treatment, though even then the aggressive form of the skin cancer can mysteriously reappear.

Christopher McDougall writes regularly for Esquire, Men's Health, *and* Bicycling *magazines. Formerly an overseas correspondent for the Associated Press, McDougall spent months in Africa reporting on the massacres in Rwanda and civil war in Angola. He won the Clarion Award in 2002.*

There are basically two types of skin cancer—lethal and disfiguring. The lethal kind is melanoma. It killed [musician] Bob Marley and [actor] Burgess Meredith, and might have killed [quarterback] Troy Aikman at the start of the 1998 NFL season and [U.S. senator] John McCain during the 2000 presidential campaign if they hadn't been saved by speedy surgery. Worldwide, one person will die of melanoma every hour, because the disease is fast and extremely aggressive: Once it penetrates your skin and enters your bloodstream, it can travel with nightmarish nimbleness, attacking your brain and every other organ in a matter of weeks.

Basal-cell and squamous-cell carcinomas, on the other hand, very rarely kill. They're the disfiguring type of skin cancer, munching away at your face and chest and arms like a flesh-eating virus. Left untreated for too long, they can cost you chunks of your ears, cheeks, chest, and arms. Nearly 1 million Americans have basal-cell carcinoma, and if you add in cases of squamous cell and melanoma, skin malignancies rank as the most common cancer in the United States.

They're also among the most predictable cancers, usually attacking older, fair-skinned people who've spent decades under blazing rays. Or at least that used to be the profile. Dermatologists have recently noticed that a rising number of their cancer patients are remarkably young. "It's becoming a regular occurrence: A 30-year-old has a red spot on his cheek that doesn't go away, and he can't believe what I have to tell him," says Roger Ceilley, M.D., who has observed legions of suntanned teens and sunbaked farmers in his dual roles as a practicing specialist and clinical professor of dermatology at the University of Iowa. Another dermatologist in Boston, David Home, M.D., adds, "I recently treated an 18-year-old with skin cancer, which would have been unheard of 10, 20 years ago."

Last August [2005], researchers at the Mayo Clinic confirmed in the lab what Dr. Ceilley and other dermatologists have been seeing in the field: Skin-cancer rates are shooting up among people under 40. According to the study, only 18 out of every 100,000 Americans under age 40 were diagnosed with basal-cell carcinoma in the 1970s; today, that rate has jumped to nearly 30 per 100,000. Squamous cell has become even more prevalent: It has quadrupled in the under-40 population. Formerly afflicting one in every 100,000 people, it now attacks four per 100,000.

This new battlefield in the war on cancer has emerged just when other key fronts are reporting progress. Leukemia, lung cancer, and colon cancer are all on the decline, thanks to medication, prevention, and early detection, but rates of melanoma—which should be the easiest cancer to prevent and detect—have nearly doubled over the past decade. The outbreaks have become so prevalent that the Skin Cancer Foundation estimates that within the next 5 years, one in every 50 Americans will have melanoma.

"These are truly frightening developments," says Randall K. Roenigk, M.D, coauthor of the Mayo Clinic study and chairman of the department of dermatology at the clinic's college of medicine, in Rochester, Minnesota. "Something that is largely preventable not only has become epidemic, but also keeps on accelerating." Dr. Roenigk thought he'd lost the capacity for surprise by the time he'd finished compiling data for the study, but even he was startled when he recently found skin cancer gnawing at the nose of a patient—who was only 12 years old.

Deadly Suntans

Unlike the mysterious origins of most diseases, tracing this epidemic back to its beginning is fairly simple: The seeds were sown 50 years ago, most likely in California, when suntans went from stigma to fashion statement. Before that, a ruddy bronze glow was mostly reserved for farmhands and stevedores. "It used to be associated with the lower classes, the laborers," says Dr. Home. "Only in our lifetime have people begun lying in the sun to 'improve' their appearances—and now they're paying for it."

We could also be paying the price for abusing the environment as badly as we've abused our skin, Dr. Home adds. "If the ozone layer is thinning as rapidly as some believe, then increased ultraviolet [UV] intensity would certainly be a factor," he says. "We haven't been measuring the UV index for very long, so it's impossible to say whether the increased cancer rates come from more exposure—more people spending more time in the sun—or a greenhouse effect, but it could be a combination of both."

But whether we're being punished for neglecting nature or ourselves, men are taking the brunt of the hit. You might think of female skin as being more delicate and consequently more vulnerable, but the truth is, men face a much higher skin-cancer risk than women. We're twice as likely to develop basal-cell or squamous-cell cancer and significantly more prone to melanoma (a one-in-58 chance, as opposed to one in 82 for women) Men are also more likely to die of melanoma, with an estimated 4,910 succumbing last year, compared with 2,860 women.

Breasts are the major reason men are more susceptible. Because guys don't have them, they spend more time shirtless in the sun, "Melanoma in men is most common on the upper back, where it can grow deep and thick," explains Diane Berson, M.D., an assistant professor of dermatology at Cornell University's Weill Medical College. "That's not surprising, when you consider that from an early age, they're outside with their shirts off cutting the lawn, raking leaves, playing sports. They can have melanoma for a long time and think it's only a freckle."

Two Male Victims

Chris Dale's sister Amanda had seen that mole on his scalp for years, ever since Chris got his hair buzzed high and tight for the army. But it wasn't until the spring of 2004, after she'd taken a "skin-care essentials" class in her massage-therapy school, that she realized it could be more than a birthmark and began nagging him about seeing a dermatologist.

Chris must've told Amanda a million times that he couldn't afford a doctor's bill. He'd just been discharged from the military because of his bad knees, and at 24, he was still working only part-time for the sheriff's office and not yet eligible for health-care coverage.

Besides, the army docs had scoped him out from tip to toe when he was inducted the year before, and even more thoroughly when he was medically discharged 6 months later. He wasn't any big sun worshipper, either. Sure, he'd hung out at the beach—after all, he lived in St. Augustine, Florida, and spent a few childhood years in the U.S. Virgin Islands, thanks to his dad's National Park Service job. But if he was spending a day in the sun, it was usually in a wool uniform. Chris had been a war buff since he was barely out of diapers, shooting his own black-powder musket by the time he was 5 and using his vacation time to attend Civil War reenactments. Besides, he snorted to his sister, he didn't even have a tan; his skin was as pale as his white T-shirt, and when he patrolled the beach on his sheriff's department ATV, he slathered on plenty of sunscreen.

"But Amanda, being a Scorpio and an older sister, had to have the last word," says Pattie Dale, Chris's mom. "She said she'd pay for it herself, and even make the appointment with her dermatologist." Chris grumbled his way to the doctor's office, and sure enough, it was just a benign birthmark. "Nothing to worry about," the doctor said.

But the next day, the doctor called back. He'd had the mole biopsied, just to be sure, and discovered he'd made a mistake. Chris had melanoma.

Meanwhile, up in New York City, John Flanagan was planning a getaway to the Hamptons. All you'd need is a glimpse of his blond Hollywood shag and wraparound midnight shades to guess that John would never miss winters in the Caribbean or summer weekends on an exclusive beach. Right before he left, though, he surrendered to his girlfriend's urging and went to have that little spot on his cheek checked out by a dermatologist.

At 40, and with a creamy, Irish-English complexion, John figured that an age spot or two was inevitable. He'd done his bit to stall time with high-end moisturizers, but he knew the years he'd spent in Los Angeles must have taken a toll on his skin. Back then, he rarely went to work without having spent at least an hour by the pool, just soaking in the warmth and thinking about his buddies shivering in the perpetual shadow of Manhattan high-rises.

Now that John was back in New York, he barely even saw the sun for weeks at a time. He made his living raising cash for film and real-estate projects, which meant lots of late-night networking in exclusive clubs and a workday that usually began when the sun was sinking. He'd gotten a bit of a burn at his weekend place in Woodstock, though, so he figured it made sense to check with a doctor about sunscreens before he hit the beach.

"Yes," the dermatologist agreed. "You'll need to get that spot scraped and biopsied."

Scraped? Guess again, doc. No way John was going to show up in the Hamptons with a gash on his face, looking like he'd been clawed in a bar fight. He'd deal with it as soon as he got back.

A Suspect Gene in Men

A single forgetful day can be all it takes to endanger your life, warns William Gallagher, Ph.D., the lead scientist of a groundbreaking new study examining why men are more likely than women to die of melanoma. If you neglect to smear on SPF one time, you're already at risk: One blistering sunburn in childhood can more than double your chances of developing the disease.

Last year, Gallagher's team at the UCD Conway Institute of Biomolecular and Biomedical Research, in Dublin, began examining the DNA of cancer cells from a young man with melanoma. What they discovered was an association between aggressive melanoma and an odd mutation that exists only on a gene in the Y chromosome—which, of course, is present only in males. "It's a striking, very strange gene," Gallagher explains by phone from Ireland. "If the gene is turned off, you appear to have thick, aggressive melanoma tumors. If it's turned on, you tend to have thinner, nonaggressive melanomas."

The thicker the melanoma tumor, the slimmer your hopes of survival. Thickness is ranked on an escalating scale from Level 1 to Level 5, and the chances of beating even Level 3 or Level 4 melanoma are only about 10 percent.

"Men really have a double whammy, because another feature of more aggressive melanoma is drug resistance," Gallagher adds. "So not only is it spreading more rapidly, but it's also far more difficult to treat."

Gallagher's next challenge is finding out whether the gene is actually a trigger or just a red flag that goes up when the melanoma mechanism is activated. And if it is a trigger, as his evidence suggests, what role do the sun's rays play in tripping it? Is there a specific amount of ultraviolet light that can flip the switch?

Ultraviolet light has already been established as the prime mover in less-lethal forms of skin cancer. According to the Skin Cancer Foundation, more than 90 percent of all skin cancers are caused by sun exposure, while regular sun protection throughout childhood can reduce the risk of the disease by a staggering 80 percent. "Your DNA actually gets broken when sunlight hits the cell," says Dr. Roenigk. "That's all a suntan is—broken cells trying to rebuild themselves. But over time, the damaged cells get tired and don't rebuild themselves as well."

So, once again, technology rides to the rescue—tanning beds are the answer, right? "They're actually more dangerous," says David Goldberg, M.D., a Manhattan-based dermatologist and vice president of the Skin Cancer Foundation. "They're terrible." One misconception is the notion that tanning beds are safer than natural light because they don't cause sunburns. "There are two types of UV light—A and B. Type B causes burns, but type A actually penetrates deeper and causes more long-term damage. And it's type A you find in tanning beds," Dr. Goldberg explains. "That is one industry that's long overdue for regulation."

If you're fair-skinned, you should actually be thankful for the burn warning UVB light provides. "Darker-complected men who don't burn think they're invincible," says Dr. Berson. True, they do have a natural advantage, since melanin—the pigment in our skin—helps screen the deeper layers of the epidermis. But your Sicilian granddad doesn't *guarantee you* unlimited nude-beach privileges. Just because your skin tans more gently doesn't mean it isn't being invisibly damaged.

"At least a lighter-skinned person gets the heads-up of a sunburn once in a while and takes precautions," says Dr. Berson. "But you'll find other men outside all the time with their shirts off, who could be slowly developing something that goes undetected until it's too late."

Fighting Back

In July 2004, a few weeks after he learned he had Level 2 melanoma, Chris Dale submitted to the scalpel again. His dermatologist had previously removed the surface layers of his mole, but now that they knew it was malignant, a surgeon would cut deep into Chris's scalp and try to slice out every trace of the tumor before it spread.

"I'm going to beat this," Chris said, and he wasn't just being defiant. He was young, and the disease had been caught when it was only a few layers deep. Plus, Chris was taking all the right steps, no matter how painful. He was scheduled to begin training as a corrections officer that autumn, but he decided to start chemo right away, even though it meant he'd be nauseated and exhausted.

Chris injected the drugs at night, hoping to sleep off the effects, but he still had to stagger through many days at the academy. Somehow, he fought through; he became one of the top marksmen in his class and was appointed squad leader.

And, come October 2004, he received an even better reward: A CT scan showed that his body was tumor-free. Thrilled, Chris and his fiancée, Mandy, began planning their wedding. They'd have it next fall, they decided, after he graduated from the corrections academy and began full-time work with the sheriff's office. "You never saw a guy with a bigger Howdy Doody grin," one of his instructors recalled.

About that time, up in New York, John Flanagan was making a second visit to his dermatologist. Again, the doctor insisted that John needed to have his sun spot analyzed, but there was something he just couldn't make the doctor understand: John always spent Christmas on St. Bart's. Seriously, how could he go walking around one of the world's toniest island resorts with some thuggish-looking bandage on his face?

Besides, the spot didn't look any worse, so what was the hurry? He'd deal with it when he got back.

Spotting the Tumors

Luckily, a fantastic device that can detect early-stage skin cancer has already been invented. You've got one, in fact.

"Men look at themselves in the mirror every day when they shave," says Dr. Roenigk. "Don't they notice that spot on their face and wonder, Hey, where'd that come from? Of all the cancers, this is the only one you can actually see."

And yet denial can be blinding. Dr. Roenigk once treated a man in his 40s with a tumor nearly 9 inches long on his chest. The man came in only because his golf club banned him from the showers—he was bleeding all over the towels. What that golfer lacked in self-preservation and basic hygiene, he made up for in luck: The tumor was basal cell, not melanoma, so even though it had penetrated between his ribs, he survived.

Caught early enough, melanoma is a relatively easy cancer to control, because it can be attacked without having to open the skull or operate around delicate internal organs. But control isn't the same as a cure; surgery and chemotherapy can usually wipe out the tumors, but only temporarily. Melanoma is notoriously tenacious and a constant threat to reappear, so the best you can hope for is a tie, never outright victory.

Long-term solutions could be available within the next few years, but only on the precondition of early detection. Gallagher is experimenting with decitabine, a medication he believes may reactivate the non-aggressive-melanoma gene in men. "We're hoping to find a focused dosage that could be viewed as a prototype," he says "In our experiments with mice, we've been able to dramatically reduce the size of the tumor and almost eradicate it."

A custom-made melanoma vaccine may also be on the way from the U.S.-based company Antigenics. Currently in late-stage testing, Oncophage is created from a patient's own melanoma tumor: Doctors extract a supply of "heat-shock proteins," a type of protein produced, when cells are under extreme stress. Because heat-shock proteins contain antigens, injecting them back into the bloodstream signals the immune system to attack the tumor cells—and leave healthy cells alone. Oncophage isn't nearly powerful enough to destroy entire tumors, but it could be an antidote against recurrences. Once the melanoma has been surgically removed, the vaccine could help the immune system overwhelm new tumors before they have a chance to develop, says John Kirkwood, M.D., the director of the melanoma center at the University of Pittsburgh Cancer Institute. "Men's ears should be perking up, because of their heightened risk."

Curiously, sunlight may also reduce melanoma's capacity to kill. According to researchers at Memorial Sloan-Kettering Cancer Center, a study of 528 patients with early-stage melanoma shows that those who'd had the most sun prior to diagnosis stood a better chance of survival. One plausible theory is that vitamin D, produced by exposure to the sun, helps slow the spread of cancer. Another possibility is that the sunlight breaks down collagen in the skin, turning it into a barrier that blocks the melanoma from penetrating into the blood or lymphatic system. But whatever the explanation, it's still a painfully weak blessing: Better to avoid excess sun and never get cancer in the first place than hope a few more rays will blunt it.

"At this point, you can't hope to outguess melanoma and head it off at the pass," says Gallagher. "It may disappear and lie dormant for years, then reappear with frightening voraciousness. There are two things you can never underestimate about skin cancer: speed and unpredictability."

Deadly Recurrence

In May 2005, Chris and Mandy had to change their wedding plans. He'd gone in for another CT scan, and the tumors that had vanished 9 months before had suddenly reappeared throughout his body. "It was bizarre," says Mandy. "He suddenly had lumps on top of lumps."

By the time the radiologists were finished counting, they'd discovered 70 tumors in Chris's abdomen, brain, lymph nodes . . . everywhere. He was immediately started on the most powerful barrage of chemotherapy his oncologist thought Chris could survive, including the newest and most aggressive protocol available, a regimen of high-dose interleukin-2. His family scrambled to put together a wedding for Chris and Mandy in 5 days; no matter what, the couple was determined to keep on living, and fighting.

Chris made it to his 25th birthday. On October 9, he was wheeled from the hospital to a surprise birthday party, where his friends and "family" from the sheriff's department turned out by the hundreds to wish him well and cheer him on. "I've got too much to live for," Chris told his kid brother, a soldier who'd rushed home from duty in South Korea to make the party. Two weeks later, Chris died.

"I still can't believe it," Mandy says. "To go from a mole to a funeral home—it's so strange. When I tell people what killed

Chris, they go, 'A mole? How can a mole kill anyone?' They see all these ads and fundraisers for breast cancer and don't realize that it isn't nearly as lethal as skin cancer."

Somehow, John Flanagan got the break that Chris Dale couldn't find. The same month that Chris and Mandy were being married in a hasty, death-cheating wedding on the beach of St. Augustine, John was finally having a biopsy performed. The doctor found melanoma on his back and basal-cell carcinoma on his face and arm.

"I have an 8-inch scar on my back," John Flanagan tells me one afternoon in New York. He also has a bandage beneath his eye and another on his arm. "Every aspect of my life is changed," he says. It's not the scars that worry him; it's the loneliness of being an early prophet in a world that has yet to get the message about melanoma. "If I want to run or play tennis, or my girlfriend wants to go to the beach, what do I do?" John asks "You know what America is like—we associate a tan with being healthy and successful. So I'm going to spend my life as the pasty-faced guy?"

He doesn't wait for an answer. "I know the alternative."

Risk Factors for Lung Cancer

Claudia I. Henschke, Peggy McCarthy, and Sarah Wernick

For many years the question of whether smoking causes lung cancer was controversial. In the 1950s the scientific community began to see convincing evidence of a link. However, another four decades would pass before the tobacco companies conceded that their product is dangerous. In the following selection, physician Claudia I. Henschke, who specializes in imaging disorders of the chest, and her coauthors describe the role of smoking and other factors in the prevalence of lung cancer. While acknowledging that smoking is by far the biggest risk factor, they identify some others, such as the naturally occurring radioactive gas radon or the now-obsolete insulating material asbestos.

Claudia I. Henschke heads the division of chest imaging at the New York Presbyterian-Cornell Medical Center. Peggy McCarthy is president of McCarthy Medical Marketing, Inc., and is founder of the Alliance for Lung Cancer Advocacy, Support, and Education. Sarah Wernick is an award-winning health writer.

Anyone can get lung cancer. However, the odds are much higher for some people than for others. Are you at risk? The answer depends in part upon your exposure to carcinogens—cancer-causing chemicals (especially those in tobacco smoke) and radiation. But that's not the whole story. You've probably heard about people who manage to celebrate their hundredth birthday in excellent heath, despite smoking a pack a day. These folks do *not* prove that cigarettes are good for you! But they underscore the fact that risk involves personal vulnerability—for example, your genetic heritage and respiratory health—as well as exposure to carcinogens. . . .

We'll also tell you about many ways to reduce your lung cancer risk, from limiting exposure to carcinogens to making healthy lifestyle changes.

Smoking is by far the most significant cause of lung cancer, accounting about 85 percent of all cases. Tobacco smoke contains at least fifty-five known carcinogens. Twenty of these—including benzopyrene, chromium, N-nitrosamine, cadmium, nickel, and arsenic—have been linked to lung cancer in animals or humans. Your lung cancer risk is closely correlated with your smoking history.

Estimating Tobacco Exposure

The measure most commonly used to summarize smoking history is the *pack-year*, the equivalent of smoking one pack of cigarettes per day for a year. For instance, if you've been smoking for ten years, and have always smoked two packs a day, your smoking history is 20 pack-years. Most smokers aren't that consistent. So you might need a few minutes to do the calculations.

When researchers want to study people at elevated risk for lung cancer, they usually recruit individuals with a smoking history of at least 10 to 20 pack-years. But smoking behavior is also relevant to risk. Two people with the same pack-year history may not have the same exposure to cigarette carcinogens. For example, one person's exposure may be greater because he or she inhales more deeply and always smokes cigarettes down to the very end, while the other typically puffs lightly and stubs out quickly.

Regardless what or how you smoke, quitting helps. The odds slowly improve with each smoke-free year, though ex-smokers always have a significantly greater risk of developing lung cancer than those who never smoked. . . .

Other Kinds of Smoking

Tobacco cigarettes are not the only problem. Other smoked products also carry significant health risks, including lung cancer.

- Cigars and pipe tobacco contain the same carcinogenic compounds found in cigarettes. Though cigar and pipe smokers have lower rates of lung cancer than cigarette smokers do, that's because they usually light up less frequently and are less likely to inhale. However, when people accustomed to cigarettes switch to cigars or pipes, they tend to inhale, often without realizing it.

- Marijuana produces the same kind of damage to the lungs that cigarette smoke does. That's not surprising: marijuana cigarettes contain more tar than tobacco cigarettes—and they're not filtered. Though marijuana smokers typically consume fewer cigarettes than tobacco smokers do, they inhale deeply and hold the smoke in their lungs.

- Bidis and kreteks, exotic flavored cigarettes, are unknown to many adults but alarmingly popular among middle and high school students. Many youngsters believe they're safer than regular cigarettes. Not so. Both are just as addictive and carry all the same health risks, including lung cancer. Bidis, which aren't filtered, are especially dangerous: since they're more loosely packed than typical American cigarettes, the smoker must puff harder and more frequently to keep them lit.

- Herbal cigarettes, which are sometimes sold in health food stores, may contain tobacco. Even if they don't, they have similar levels of tar and their smoke contains many of the same kinds of irritants as tobacco cigarettes. Though their health hazards haven't been researched, they can be presumed to carry a risk for lung cancer.

Secondhand Smoke and Other Risks

If you spend time with people who smoke, you're exposed to secondhand smoke—a mix of "mainstream" smoke exhaled by smokers and "sidestream" smoke from burning tobacco. The chemical composition of both kinds of secondhand smoke is similar to what smokers inhale. The Environmental Protection Agency estimates that 3,000 nonsmokers per year develop lung cancer because they're exposed to other people's tobacco smoke at home or at work. The thicker the cloud, the greater the risk. . . .

Carcinogens are all around us. We can't escape them entirely, but we can nearly always reduce our exposure. That's important because many carcinogens are *synergistic*. In other words, when you're exposed to more than one, their effects don't merely add up—they multiply. Here are the carcinogens most relevant to lung cancer risk:

Radon Gas

The leading cause of lung cancer in nonsmokers is radon—a colorless, odorless radioactive gas that is found in soil. We've known that radon can cause lung cancer ever since the 1930s, when a colleague of Claudia Henschke's father made the connection in Czechoslovakian miners. Miners are still at risk. But we now know that they're not alone. Radon can seep into buildings and accumulate in poorly ventilated rooms. If this happens in your home, you could inhale dangerous amounts.

In the lungs, radon releases tiny bursts of radiation that can damage lung tissue and lead to cancer. The risk is much greater for smokers. According to the Environmental Protection Agency (EPA), radon contributes to up to 10,000 lung cancer deaths annually. . . .

Medical X-Rays

When radon is inhaled or radiation is directed to the chest, lung cancer risk is increased. If your job requires you to wear a radiation badge, you know you're exposed at work and need to observe safety precautions.

For most of us, the best way to minimize radiation exposure is to avoid unnecessary medical x-rays. However, in many instances, the benefits outweigh the risks. X-rays are valuable tools for diagnosing injuries or illnesses; they're also used for treatment. Fortunately, current techniques have greatly reduced unnecessary radiation exposure to the lungs during cancer therapy. But several studies have found an elevated incidence of lung cancer in breast cancer survivors who received radiation treatments long ago; within this group, the risk is significantly higher for smokers. While long-term survivors need to know about the risk—especially if they smoke—this threat is much less for today's patients.

Asbestos

Asbestos is a mineral that was widely used in construction and manufacturing from the 1940s to the 1970s. When asbestos is crushed, it breaks into tiny fibers. If these fibers are inhaled, they may damage the lungs. The effects usually are seen only decades later.

People exposed to asbestos in their work have a much higher than normal incidence of lung cancer. This includes people involved in asbestos mining and manufacture, as well as those who work with asbestos-containing products such as brakes or insulation. The risk is greatly compounded for individuals who smoke. Nonsmokers exposed to asbestos are ten times more likely to get lung cancer than other nonsmokers—but for smokers with similar asbestos exposure, the risk is *ninety* times higher.

Though asbestos is used much less now than in the past, many older buildings contain asbestos products, such as insulation, shingles, or floor tile. If these are in good condition, they pose no significant risk to occupants. But dangers arise if old asbestos deteriorates and begins to crumble, or if dust is raised by renovations or repairs. . . .

Experts estimate that each year 10,000 to 12,000 Americans develop lung cancer from exposure to carcinogens at work. The culprits include hazardous chemicals, as well as asbestos, radon, radiation, and secondhand smoke. The dangers are particularly great for smokers who are also exposed to these substances.

One Worker's Story

I worked for the county government, in an old warehouse that had a smell like rotten eggs. The vents were full of black soot. People were being diagnosed with cancer, one after another.

The county hired someone to do a study. They declared the building perfectly safe and said, "Forget about it." We didn't forget about it. We tracked who got cancer and where they sat. There were about seven hundred people in the building. Over the previous ten years, there had been one cancer diagnosis every three months. I worked in one area where there was a cancer cluster. We later learned that herbicides and pesticides had been stored right above the floor where we were working.

I was diagnosed with lung cancer in 1997. I'm not a scientist, and I can't prove that the building was the cause of my cancer. I was a former smoker, which put me at risk. I loved my work, but I took early retirement because I didn't want to return to that building.

—*Joyce*

Air Pollution

If the air you breathe every day irritates your eyes and makes you cough, it's probably harming your lungs. Chronic exposure to air pollution has been linked to lung cancer, as well as to asthma, chronic bronchitis, and emphysema. . . .

Family History

If you have a family history of lung cancer—your parents or siblings have had the disease—you are at higher risk. The association can be explained in part by shared environmental hazards, such as exposure to tobacco smoke and other pollutants in the home. But careful studies that take account of these issues suggest that genetic factors are at work too. Indeed, in specific subgroups of lung cancer patients—including those who develop the disease early and nonsmoking women with adenocarcinoma [a malignant tumor]—the association with family history is greater than it is for breast, ovarian, colon, or prostate cancer. . . .

Higher Risk in Women

Until the 1960s, lung cancer was rare in women. But a time bomb was ticking: during the 1940s, increasing numbers of women had taken up smoking. Twenty years later, in the 1960s, the explosive rise of women's lung cancer began. In just three decades, deaths more than quadrupled. In 1987, for the first time, more women died from lung cancer than from breast cancer. Every year since then, the gap has grown wider, as breast cancer fatalities slowly drop while women's lung cancer deaths continue to rise.

Trends in smoking only partly account for this epidemic. Mounting research evidence suggests that women are more vulnerable to tobacco carcinogens than men are. For example, Claudia Henschke's first CT [Computed Tomography] screening project recruited 541 men and 459 women who had no symptoms of lung cancer but who were at high risk. Since there were more men than women in the study, they expected more men among those with lung cancer. In fact, there were almost three times as many women as men. Other studies have reported similar findings.

Women clearly are at higher risk, but why? We have some tantalizing leads, but we won't know the full story until more research has been done. Estrogen appears to play a role. Genetic factors may be involved too. A University of Pittsburgh study put the spotlight on a gene called the gastrin-releasing peptide receptor gene (GRPR), which is more active in women than in men—and which also is linked to abnormal cell growth in the lungs. And a study from the M.D. Anderson Cancer Center suggests that the capacity to repair DNA may be lower in women than in men.

Risk in African American Men

African-American men have especially high rates of lung cancer. The incidence of the disease is one and a half times higher among black men than it is among white men. Though scientists have struggled to explain this extraordinary discrepancy, the reasons are not fully understood. Adding to the mystery is the fact that African-American women have only very slightly higher lung cancer rates than do their white counterparts.

One explanation is that African-American men are more likely to smoke than white men. Moreover, they're much more likely to smoke mentholated cigarettes. But we're not sure if that's significant. On the one hand, when menthol burns, it produces additional carcinogens. However, some research suggests that menthol doesn't really make much difference. And the smoking patterns of black men aren't different enough to account for the racial gap in lung cancer rates.

Also relevant is the fact that African-American men suffer from greater exposure to air pollution. They're more likely than white men to live in cities, and to hold industrial jobs that involve toxic dusts. Diet could be a factor. African-American men consume more fat and fewer fruits and vegetables than white men, a pattern linked to higher rates of lung cancer. Yet another possibility is that there's some genetic difference that makes for greater vulnerability.

The Role of Diet and Hormones in Breast Cancer

Bonnie Liebman

Breast cancer is the number one form of cancer affecting women in America, according to author Bonnie Liebman. In some countries, such as Japan, the malady is comparatively rare. That has led scientists to suspect a lifestyle link, and extensive studies suggest that diet plays a role. The U.S. diet tends to be long on red meat and short on fresh fruits and vegetables. Moreover, American women tend to be considerably heavier than Japanese women. That extra fat may be the difference, Liebman indicates. Fat cells exude hormones that are suspected of being triggers for breast cancer. However, large-scale studies show that the risk can be mitigated by regular exercise.

Bonnie Liebman is nutrition director for the Center for Science in the Public Interest. The nonprofit center advocates for government policies and corporate practices that promote healthy diets, prevent deceptive marketing practices, and ensure that science is used to promote the public welfare.

An estimated 211,000 American women will be diagnosed with breast cancer this year [2005]. The disease will kill 40,000. The only cancer that will kill more women (73,000) is lung.

Yet high breast cancer rates aren't universal. North America leads the pack, followed closely by Europe and other industrialized regions. Lower rates are found almost exclusively in developing countries. The exception: Japan.

Japanese women are only one-third as likely as American women to get breast cancer. But genes don't explain the difference, because the risk rises when Japanese women emigrate to the U.S., and rates in Japan have been rising (they used to be one-fifth of ours).

What is it about the U.S. diet, environment, or lifestyle that accounts for the discrepancy? That question has fueled much of the research on preventing breast cancer for the last 30 years. Here's what researchers have found so far.

Fatty Foods

Could fatty foods promote breast cancer? Researchers seized on fat as a culprit in the 1970s, in trying to explain why Japanese women were much less likely to get breast cancer than American women. The Japanese were getting only 10 percent of their calories from fat, far less than the typical 40 percent that U.S. women were eating.

But the link between breast cancer and fatty foods didn't hold up as researchers gathered more precise data, especially when they pooled data in 2001 from studies that tracked more than 350,000 women.

With blame shifting away from fatty foods, "we thought that Asian women had a lower risk of breast cancer because they consumed fewer calories, had a lower body weight, or were more physically active than American women," says cancer researcher Regina Ziegler of the National Cancer Institute in Bethesda, Maryland.

But the spotlight turned back to fat last May [2005], when researchers reported that a low-fat diet (20 percent of calories) cut the risk of recurring breast cancers in a study of more than 2,400 postmenopausal women who had already undergone the usual medical treatment for early-stage breast cancer.

The low-fat eaters averaged only 33 grams of fat a day, considerably less than the 51 grams a day eaten by similar breast cancer patients who were instructed to follow their usual diet.

"The low-fat group decreased their portion sizes of dairy, meat, and baked goods like sweet rolls and drastically reduced their oils and spreads," says lead investigator Rowan Chlebowski of the Los Angeles Biomedical Research Institute in Torrance, California.

"This is the first randomized clinical trial showing that diet may have an impact on breast cancer outcome."

Even more surprising: the risk of recurring breast cancer was reduced—by 42 percent—only in low-fat dieters whose original tumors weren't sensitive to estrogen. Those "estrogen-negative" cancers—which account for about a quarter of all breast cancers in the U.S.—are hard to treat because they don't respond to estrogen-blocking drugs like tamoxifen.

But experts are cautious about the results.

More Studies Needed

"The press made it sound like a clear answer, but the study has to be regarded as preliminary," says Harvard's Willett. "It hasn't been published, and they have another eight months of follow-up that weren't included in the analysis," which was presented at a scientific meeting in May.

What's more, the results were statistically significant, but just barely—that is, they were almost chalked up to chance, largely because the number of estrogen-negative cancers was small.

"I don't want to oversell results with a borderline significance," says Chlebowski. "We need to wait for more follow-up and other studies. We can't tell women that they should change what they eat or their cancer is more likely to recur."

On the other hand, it's possible that earlier studies failed to find a link between fat and breast cancer because they didn't distinguish between estrogen-negative and estrogen-positive tumors. "Until recently, we didn't have data on estrogen receptor status," says Willett. "It may turn out to be an important distinction."

Willett, his Harvard colleague David Hunter, and others recently found similar results in one of their studies. Women who reported eating a "prudent" diet pattern had a lower risk of breast cancer than those who ate a "Western" pattern, Here again, the diet link appeared only in women who were diagnosed with estrogen-negative cancers.

The prudent pattern (more fruits, vegetables, whole grains, low-fat dairy foods, fish, and poultry) is closer to the low-fat diet in Chlebowski's study than the Western pattern (more red and processed meats, refined grains, sweets, and high-fat dairy).

"It's possible that estrogen-positive tumors are so dominated by the effect of estrogen that it may mask other factors," suggests Willett. So diet may only affect estrogen-negative tumors.

Fruit and Veggies Count

And it may not be less fat, but more fruits and vegetables, that matters. "Almost all the benefit of the prudent pattern was coming from fruits and vegetables," Willett notes.

That seems to contradict the results of a study that pooled data on more than 350,000 women, which showed that fruits and vegetables had no impact on breast cancer risk. But, like earlier studies on fat, it didn't separate estrogen-negative and estrogen-positive cancers.

Experts are eagerly awaiting results from the Women's Health Initiative to see if diet can reduce the risk of breast cancer and other diseases.

"We have 48,000 otherwise-healthy postmenopausal women randomized to a typical diet or a low-fat diet with more fruits and vegetables," says Chlebowski, one of the trial's investigators. The results are due out in the first quarter of 2006.

Until researchers know more, says Hunter, "women who want to cut fat should do it by replacing much of their fat with fruits and vegetables, not by eating low-fat processed foods." Loading up on cakes, cookies, ice cream, white bread, and other foods that are often labeled "low-fat" would be a mistake.

"We have good evidence that eating more sugar and refined flour will increase the risk of obesity, diabetes, heart disease, and quite probably cancer," says Hunter. "A low-fat diet could do harm if you replace fat with those carbohydrates."

Weight and Weight Gain

For years, studies could not nail down a clear link between weight and breast cancer. Then, in the 1990s, scientists figured out why the link was so fuzzy. Among other things, it shows up:

- With modest weight gain. It's possible that weight seemed to have little impact on breast cancer in American women because the vast majority are considerably heavier than Japanese women.

But Ziegler and colleagues saw the impact of weight when they looked at Asian Americans (who weigh less than most other Americans). Asian American women who were heavier-than-average and had gained more than 10 pounds in the previous decade had three times the breast cancer risk of leaner Asian Americans.

"We may have to get much slimmer to reach the low risk of Asians," she suggests.

- Only in postmenopausal women. Being overweight doesn't raise the risk of breast cancer in premenopausal women, so any studies that mixed them in with postmenopausal women might not have detected a link.

- Only in women who don't take hormones. For years, estrogen pills obscured the link between breast cancer and weight. "We found twice the risk of breast cancer in women who gained the most weight after age 20 compared to those who kept their weight constant," says Willett, "but only when we looked at women who had never used hormone replacement therapy."

Weight Adds Estrogen

Experts believe that extra fat cells raise the risk of breast cancer because they produce hormones that the body converts to estrogen.

"Estrogen levels in the blood are three times higher in overweight women than in lean women," says Willett. "That's a huge difference."

But extra estrogen from fat cells gets swamped by the estrogen from hormone replacement pills.

Recent studies suggest that it's not just estrogen, but also androgens, that raise the risk of breast cancer in overweight women. "We think that higher circulating estrogens explains why postmenopausal women who are overweight have a higher breast cancer risk," says Ziegler, "but it's possible that other hormones are also important."

That's not to say that being overweight can make or break your chances of getting breast cancer. "Plenty of lean women get breast cancer," notes Harvard's Hunter. So, by staying trim, "you're reducing your risk, not abolishing it."

Weight Gain Stands Out

Nevertheless, the link between higher weight and the risk of postmenopausal breast cancer is "fairly strong and highly reproducible," says Willett. "It's a very important public health message."

And the risk rises long before you're shopping for plus-size clothes. "Gaining two or three pounds a year after age 18 or 20 adds up to quite a bit of excess risk by menopause," he explains. "Even a quarter of a pound a year—five to eight pounds by menopause—is a significant excess risk."

In fact, it's unusual for American women to weigh the same as they did at age 20. In a study that tracked women through the 1980s and early 1990s, "only 5 percent didn't take hormones or gain weight during adulthood," says Willett. "But in Japan, it was almost 100 percent of women, at least until recently."

On his visits to Japan, Willett has seen a different attitude toward eating than ours. "They don't have a culture of overindulging," he explains, especially among women.

As the Japanese diet becomes more Westernized, "the men have gained weight, but the women have remained remarkably lean," says Willett. "To a Japanese woman, one of the worst things that can happen is to become obese."

Exercise Helps

Does a walk a day keep breast cancer away? For years, researchers weren't sure, because exercise seemed to protect women in some studies but not others.

"In the Nurses Health Study, we had to use a 16-year follow-up of more than 85,000 women, more than 3,000 cancer cases, and repeated measures of physical activity to see a relationship with breast cancer," says Willett. "Very few studies are that powerful."

The nurses study found an 18 percent lower risk in women who reported moderate or vigorous physical activity for at least seven hours a week compared to women who exercised for less than an hour a week.

"But unless you have a very large, very long study, you could miss the association," Willett explains.

That's partly because exercise doesn't drive down risk dramatically. "Physical activity has a weaker relationship with breast cancer than with diabetes, heart disease, and colon cancer," he says.

Last June [2005], researchers reported that exercise seems to improve survival in women who already have breast cancer.

"We found the maximum benefit in women who walked the equivalent of three to five hours a week," says researcher Michelle Holmes of Harvard Medical School. They walked at an average pace—two to three miles an hour—with no benefit in walking faster or longer.

"The effect was most prominent in women whose tumors were hormone-positive," she adds. That comes as no surprise to Holmes.

"Women who are physically active have lower hormone levels, and hormones stimulate breast cancer growth," she notes. Other studies suggest that an exercise program—45 minutes a day for five days a week—can lower estrogen levels in sedentary, overweight postmenopausal women.

"Physical activity may also improve the quality of life and self-image of women who've had breast cancer," adds Holmes. And it can help women avoid weight gain.

"Patients who gain weight have a poorer survival," she notes. Of course, physical activity can also help women fend off the extra padding that boosts the risk of getting breast cancer in the first place.

Staying active can prevent so many problems that it's tough to argue against it. "You don't have a lot to lose," says Holmes, "except maybe a higher risk of diabetes and heart disease."

The Role of Alcohol

"The evidence is solid that alcohol is a small, modest risk factor," says Willett. "It's been seen in 100 studies by now."

What's small? "One drink a day is associated with an 8 to 10 percent increase in risk, and two drinks a day are associated with a 25 percent increase," he says. "That's not huge, but given that the risk for nondrinkers is high, the increase is appreciable."

It's not clear how alcohol influences the breast. Some studies suggest that it may raise estrogen levels. Willett argues that the B-vitamin folate plays a role.

"Alcohol increases the requirement for folic acid, so when you have marginal folate intake and add alcohol, you really have inadequate folate," he says.

If he's right, his studies suggest that you can dodge that excess risk just by taking a multivitamin, which usually has 400 micrograms of folic acid. "Its one of the few easy fixes," says Willett. . . .

The Hormonal Hazard

As researchers search for risk factors for breast cancer, they find a recurring theme. "One thing that's consistent is the association with estrogen," says Hunter.

For example, risk is lower in women who have at least two pregnancies, breastfeed for more than one year, or get their first menstrual period—menarche—late (at age 15 or older). What ties those risk factors together? Fewer menstrual cycles and less estrogen.

"It's natural menstrual cycles—the cycling of estrogen in combination with progestin—that really kicks up breast cancer risk because it makes cells multiply," says Willett.

Breast cells are multiplying to get ready for breastfeeding should the woman become pregnant. But until recently, those cycles were few and far between.

"Women hardly ever had a menstrual cycle, because they were pregnant or lactating throughout their premenopausal years, and then menopause came along," explains Willett. "But we've created a non-natural state in human history, where women are ovulating and cycling every month for 30 years."

Menstrual periods don't explain all risk factors. For example, having a first baby at an early age (20 or younger) also lowers the risk of breast cancer, probably because the pregnancy makes breast cells differentiate, or specialize, earlier. Once they've differentiated, estrogen may cause less damage.

Of course, American teenagers aren't about to start having more babies to lower their breast cancer risk.

"It looks like breast cancer comes with the territory of an abundant food supply, early menarche, and late age at first birth," says Hunter. "Once you get beyond the reproductive factors, we haven't found ways to influence it, apart from avoiding alcohol, weight gain, and postmenopausal hormones."

But the picture may not be as bleak as it sounds. Researchers are trying to figure out exactly how hormones or growth factors promote cancer.

"If we can understand why they're so important at the cellular level," explains [National Cancer Institute's Regina] Ziegler, "we might find out how to lower the risk without asking women to bear children early or to choose early menopause."

Pancreatic Cancer and Its Many Symptoms

Harvard Health Letter

*The pancreas is an organ that does not usually get much atten-
tion. Tucked away behind the stomach, it quietly supplies needed
enzymes for digestion and insulin for the absorption of sugar.
When cancer strikes the pancreas, it is often fatal. In the following selection, doctors and researchers from the* Harvard Health
Letter *describe recent discoveries about the nature of the disease
and means of treatment. Unfortunately, symptoms of pancreatic
cancer can be vague, but some include jaundice, abdominal discomfort, weight loss, and loss of appetite. Causes are also difficult to determine, but smoking is a well-established risk factor.
Treatment relies more heavily on radiation and chemotherapy
than some other cancers because surgery is not an option for
most people, given the way the disease starts and spreads before
it can be detected.*

The Harvard Health Letter *is a medical newsletter at Harvard Medical School. It keeps up with medical news that affects
people's health and well-being by providing facts from doctors
and researchers at Harvard Medical School.*

Treatment advances have been slow in coming. What makes
this cancer so intractable?

There's been a steady stream of good news about cancer
lately, from targeted therapies like Gleevec to new strategies
like anti-angiogenesis, which zeroes in on the proliferating
blood vessels that feed tumors. Some cancers—for example,
Hodgkin's disease, a type of lymph cancer—are increasingly
treatable. The number of Americans dying from breast and
colon cancer is decreasing.

But good news about pancreatic cancer is harder to come by. Doctors haven't yet discovered how to detect it early. Treatment has progressed some, but there's been nothing close to a breakthrough.

Now there's a move to go back to medicine's drawing board: basic research. The hope is that a better understanding of the disease's genetics and molecular-level mechanisms will reveal an Achilles' heel and a target for more effective treatment. Early detection is another goal because pancreatic cancer is rarely detected until it has spread (metastasized).

Meanwhile, like other diseases, pancreatic cancer now has advocacy and support groups that help patients and their families, raise money, and push for more research.

The Pancreas: A Hidden Organ

The pancreas has two functions—releasing fluids and enzymes into the small intestine to aid digestion, and producing hormones (mainly insulin and glucagon) that are instrumental to the body's use of sugar.

Only about 10% of pancreatic cancers occur in the hormone-producing, or endocrine, tissues known as the islets of Langerhans.

Far more common are cancers that originate in the tissues that produce and deliver enzymes and digestive fluids. These exocrine cancers, as they're called, can develop in any part of the pancreas, although most (60%) start in the head of the organ, which nestles up against the curved upper portion of the small intestine.

Symptoms Can Be Vague

Occasionally the disease does produce symptoms that serve as an early warning. A tumor in the head of the pancreas can pinch off the bile duct, so bilirubin from the liver and gallbladder back up into the bloodstream. The resulting yellow discoloration of the skin and eyes—jaundice—accounts for the majority of diagnoses that occur soon enough for surgery.

But many times, in its early stages, pancreatic cancer doesn't cause any symptoms. Those that do occur—abdominal discomfort, weight loss, not being hungry—can be mistaken for indigestion or some other minor gastrointestinal problem.

Not Many Risk Factors

Smoking is one well-established risk factor. Smokers are two to three times more likely to get pancreatic cancer than non-smokers are. Some studies have implicated high-fat diets.

Pancreatic cancer is clearly linked to some forms of chronic pancreatitis, which has various causes, including alcohol abuse. But whether there's a connection between alcoholism and pancreatic cancer is far from clear. If there is one, it doesn't seem to be very strong.

Isolated cases of acute pancreatitis, such as those caused by gallstones, don't appear to increase risk for the disease.

Incidence Is Holding Steady

Eleventh among cancers in the number of new cases diagnosed each year (the incidence), pancreatic cancer isn't the most common type of cancer. It is, though, one of the deadliest, ranking fourth among cancers in the number of deaths it causes. The median survival time is about six months. Fewer than one in every five Americans diagnosed with the disease will be living a year later.

One bright spot is that its incidence has been level despite demographic trends that would tend to pull it up.

Like many cancers, pancreatic cancer is an older person's disease: 80% of those diagnosed with it are older than 60. Because of increased longevity and the aging of the baby boom generation, the number of older Americans is growing rapidly.

Yet over the past several decades, its incidence has been steady: 11 to 12 new cases diagnosed each year per 100,000 Americans. (In absolute numbers, that meant 33,730 new cases in 2006, according to the American Cancer Society estimate.) The declining number of smokers may be offsetting the aging population.

Breakthroughs Wanted

Pancreatic cancer can be treated surgically by removing the tumor if the cancer hasn't spread to blood vessels, distant lymph nodes, other organs—a big if, given that it's so often diagnosed late. Fewer than 20% of pancreatic tumors can be removed surgically.

A major change in treatment occurred with the introduction of the chemotherapy drug gemcitabine (Gemzar) for postsurgical use. Gemcitabine (pronounced jem-SITE-a-bean) is in a class of medications known as antimetabolites that work by interfering with cancer cell growth. It's used after surgery to keep the cancer from coming back.

Findings reported by a German group in January 2007 in the Journal of the American Medical Association bolstered arguments that using gemcitabine might be preferable to the standard postsurgical treatment in this country, which involves using radiation and an older drug, 5-fluorouracil (5-FU). Using gemcitabine after radiation and 5-FU may benefit some patients. But experts have been debating the nuances of postsurgical treatment for years and will continue to do so. Sadly, the bottom line is that no matter how treatments are mixed and matched, about 75% of patients who have surgery will die of recurrent disease within three to four years.

Combining drugs, often in a one-two punch, has worked with some cancers. Researchers have tried that approach with pancreatic cancer. Over a dozen studies have teamed gemcitabine up with other drugs, including some of the brand-new agents like bevacizumab (Avastin), an anti-angiogenesis drug, and erlotinib (Tarceva). The results have been disappointing.

One reason that pancreatic cancer may be so hard to treat is that the pancreas is not encased in a membrane as other organs are. This "nakedness" may make local spread more likely. In addition, pancreatic tumors also get cocooned in scarlike tissue that creates a low-oxygen environment, which makes radiation and chemotherapy less effective. Lastly, the genes of pancreatic cancer cells have multiple mutations, which may be why they can fend off chemotherapy drugs so well.

Gain Against Pain

When pancreatic cancer can't be treated surgically, doctors do their best to ameliorate symptoms and help people live a little longer.

If, for example, the pancreatic tumor is obstructing the bile duct or gastric outlet, doctors can open the blockage with a stent or surgical bypass.

Pain can be managed in a number of ways. Opioids (such as fentanyl, morphine, and oxycodone) are highly effective. Doctors are having success with injections of alcohol into (or around) nerves near the pancreas.

Chemotherapy and radiation may also be part of palliative care, as it is called, reducing pain and other symptoms by shrinking the size of the tumor. Gemcitabine is beneficial in this regard.

Genetic Studies

Pancreatic cancer does run in some families. One example is former President Jimmy Carter's family: His father and a brother and sister died of pancreatic cancer.

Researchers have also found that pancreatic cancer is more common in families with several rare inherited cancer syndromes (Peutz-Jeghers to name one) that until recently weren't associated with the disease. Researchers have recently made the intriguing discovery that mutations in the BRCA2 gene, first identified as a breast and ovarian cancer gene, may also be a causative factor in pancreatic cancer. Gloria Petersen, a Mayo Clinic researcher, is creating a large national pancreatic cancer registry in hopes of identifying more genes associated with the disease.

In December 2006, the field of pancreatic cancer genetics got its most exciting news in years: Research published in the online journal PLoS Medicine identified the first gene specifically implicated as a cause of pancreatic cancer—a mutated palladin gene.

The palladin gene produces a protein that makes up the cell walls (the name is a reference to the Renaissance architect Andrea Palladio). The protein generated by the mutated version may permit those cells to move faster than normal cells, which could explain why pancreatic cancer spreads so rapidly to other parts of the body.

Other genetic abnormalities that accompany pancreatic cancer include mutations of the K-ras gene (found in 90% of pancreatic cancers) and the p53 tumor cell suppressor gene (found in 50%–70%).

Early Detection

An especially exciting area of research involves the search for substances that could aid in spotting pancreatic cancer earlier. The mutated palladin gene—or the protein it expresses— might serve as such a biomarker.

There's considerable interest in certain growth-regulating proteins—known collectively as transforming growth factor-beta (TGF-beta)—that appear to play a role in the underlying mechanism of pancreatic cancer and might be used for early diagnosis.

So far none of the imaging technologies—CT scans, MRIs, ultrasound—have been shown to work for screening. But there are ongoing studies in high-risk individuals, which may show that a combination of tests will be useful in finding abnormal growths early.

Pancreatic cancer doesn't seem to start off with a bang. "It doesn't grow that fast," says Dr. Robert Mayer, a Harvard pancreatic cancer expert. "It's just hard to identify." Researchers think there may be an extended precancerous stage when lesions known as pancreatic intraepithelial neoplasias are localized. It's possible these lesions release a protein into the blood that will be useful in screening and early detection.

Animal Models

Pancreatic cancer research has long been hampered by a lack of an animal model that mimics the human disease. Animal models allow researchers to look for new biomarkers and try untested therapies without putting humans at risk. Using a technique of cross-breeding to create genetic abnormalities similar to those in human patients, investigators at several centers, including the Dana-Farber/Harvard Cancer Center, have developed a very promising mouse model. Researchers at Johns Hopkins are working on a zebrafish model.

Ovarian Cancer and the Problem of Diagnosis

Denise Grady

Ovarian cancer is one of the most difficult types of cancer to detect. No test for ovarian cancer exists. However, in the following selection science journalist Denise Grady reports that researchers have identified a set of symptoms that may flag the disease. The ovaries are deep inside a woman's body, and therefore fewer than one in five cases of ovarian cancer are diagnosed early. Failing to detect the cancer in its early stages frequently results in the death of the victim, Grady reports. However, oncologists—the specialists who treat cancer—are hopeful that the newly identified symptoms will act as an early warning system. The symptoms include persistent bloating or quickly feeling full at mealtime, pains in the abdomen or pelvis, and a pressing need to urinate. None is a definite indicator of ovarian cancer, but if any of these symptoms continues daily for several weeks, women are advised to seek a diagnosis. Many cancer organizations have endorsed the symptom warnings. However, doctors caution that it will take time to determine how effective they are at catching the disease in its early stages.

Denise Grady is a science reporter for the New York Times. *She joined the* Times *science staff in 1998.*

Cancer experts have identified a set of health problems that may be symptoms of ovarian cancer, and they are urging women who have the symptoms for more than a few weeks to see their doctors.

The new advice is the first official recognition that ovarian cancer, long believed to give no warning until it was far advanced, does cause symptoms at earlier stages in many women.

The symptoms to watch out for are bloating, pelvic or abdominal pain, difficulty eating or feeling full quickly and feeling a frequent or urgent need to urinate. A woman who has any of those problems nearly every day for more than two or three weeks is advised to see a gynecologist, especially if the symptoms are new and quite different from her usual state of health.

Doctors say they hope that the recommendations will make patients and doctors aware of early symptoms, lead to earlier diagnosis and, perhaps, save lives, or at least prolong survival.

But it is too soon to tell whether the new measures will work or whether they will lead to a flood of diagnostic tests or even unnecessary operations.

Late Diagnosis Leads to Death

Cancer experts say it is worth trying a more aggressive approach to finding ovarian cancer early. The disease is among the deadlier types of cancer, because most cases are diagnosed late, after the cancer has begun to spread.

This year [2007], 22,430 new cases and 15,280 deaths are expected in the United States.

If the cancer is found and surgically removed early, before it spreads outside the ovary, 93 percent of patients are still alive five years later. Only 19 percent of cases are found that early, and 45 percent of all women with the disease survive at least five years after the diagnosis.

By contrast, among women with breast cancer, 89 percent survive five years or more.

The new recommendations, expected to be formally announced on June 25 [2007], are being made by the Gynecologic Cancer Foundation, the Society of Gynecologic Oncologists and the American Cancer Society.

More than 12 other groups have endorsed them, including CancerCare; Gilda's Club, a support network for anyone touched by cancer; and several medical societies.

"The majority of the time this won't be ovarian cancer, but it's just something that should be considered," said Dr. Barbara Goff, the director of gynecologic oncology at the University of Washington in Seattle and an author of several studies that helped identify the relevant symptoms.

Stand-out Symptoms

In a number of studies by Dr. Goff and other researchers, these symptoms stood out in women with ovarian cancer as compared with other women.

"We don't want to scare people, but we also want to arm people with the appropriate information," said Dr. Goff, who is also a spokeswoman for the Gynecologic Cancer Foundation.

She emphasized that relatively new and persistent problems were the most important ones. So, the transient bloating that often accompanies menstrual periods would not qualify, nor would a lifelong history of indigestion.

Dr. Goff also acknowledged that the urinary problems on the list were classic symptoms of bladder infections, which is common in women. But it still makes sense to consult a doctor, she said, because bladder infections should be treated. Urinary trouble that persists despite treatment is a particular cause for concern, she said.

With ovarian cancer, even a few months' delay in making the diagnosis may make a difference in survival, because the tumors can grow and spread quickly through the abdomen to the intestines, liver, diaphragm and other organs, Dr. Goff said.

"If you let it go for three months, you can wind up with disease everywhere," she said

A New Tool for Women

Dr. Thomas J. Herzog, director of gynecologic oncology at the Columbia University Medical Center, said the recommendations were important because the medical profession had until now told women that there were no specific early symptoms.

"If women were more pro-active at recognizing these symptoms, we'd be better at making the diagnosis at an earlier stage," Dr. Herzog said.

"These are nonspecific symptoms that many people have," he added. "But when the symptoms persist or worsen, you need to see a specialist. By no means do we want this to result in unnecessary surgery. But I would not expect that to occur in the vast majority of cases."

Although the American Cancer Society agreed to the recommendations, it did so with some reservations, said Debbie Saslow, director of breast and gynecologic cancer at the society.

"We don't have any consensus about what doctors should do once the women come to them," Dr. Saslow said. "There was a lot of hope that we'd be able to say, 'Go to your doctor, and they will give you this standardized work-up.' But we can't do that."

At the same time, Dr. Saslow said, the cancer society recognized that in some cases doctors had disregarded symptoms in women who were later found to have ovarian cancer, telling the women instead that they were just growing old or going through menopause.

"There are so many horror stories of doctors who have told women to ignore these symptoms or have even belittled them on top of that," Dr. Saslow said.

Frequent Errors

In a survey of 1,700 women with ovarian cancer, Dr. Goff and other researchers found that 36 percent had initially been given a wrong diagnosis, with conditions like depression or irritable bowel syndrome.

"Twelve percent were told there was nothing wrong with them, and it was all in their heads," Dr. Goff said.

Dr. Goff and other specialists said women with the listed symptoms should see a gynecologist for a pelvic and rectal examination. (The best way for a doctor to feel the ovaries is through the rectum.) If there is a question of cancer, the next step is probably a test called a transvaginal ultrasound to check the ovaries for abnormal growths, enlargement or telltale pockets of fluid that can signal cancer. The ultrasound costs $150 to $300 and can be performed in a doctor's office or a radiology center. A $100 blood test should also be conducted for CA125, a substance called a tumor marker that is often elevated in women with ovarian cancer.

Cancer specialists say any woman with suspicious findings on the tests should be referred to a gynecologic oncologist, a surgeon who specializes in cancers of the female reproductive system.

What Next?

An unresolved question is what exactly should be done if the test results are normal and yet the woman continues to have symptoms, Dr. Saslow said.

"Do you do exploratory surgery, which has side effects, which are sometimes even fatal?" she asked. "What do you do? We don't have the answer to that." Depending on the test results, the woman may just be monitored for a while or advised to undergo a CT scan or an MRI. But if cancer is strongly suspected, she will probably be urged to go straight to surgery. A needle biopsy, commonly used for breast lumps, cannot be safely performed to check for ovarian cancer because it runs a risk of rupturing the tumor and spreading malignant cells in the abdomen. Instead, the surgeon must carefully remove the entire ovary or the abnormal growth on it and examine the rest of the abdomen for cancer.

While the patient is still on the operating table, biopsies are performed on the tissue that was removed, so that if cancer is found, the surgeon can operate more extensively. Experts say such an operation should be carried out just by gynecologic oncologists, who have special training in meticulously removing as much of the cancerous tissue as possible. This procedure, called debulking, lets chemotherapy work better and greatly improves survival.

Screening Test Still Needed

Dr. Carol L. Brown, a gynecologic oncologist at the Memorial Sloan Kettering Cancer Center in Manhattan, said, "Ideally, we need to develop a screening tool or a test to find ovarian cancer before it has symptoms."

No such screening test exists, Dr. Brown said, and until one is developed, the list of symptoms may be the best solution.

"This is something that women themselves can do," she added, "and we can familiarize clinicians with, to help make the diagnosis earlier."

Cancer of the Lymphatic System

National Cancer Institute

Non-Hodgkins lymphoma, or NHL for short, is a form of cancer that strikes the lymphatic system. In the following selection the National Cancer Institute describes the body's lymphatic system and its vulnerability to cancer. The lymph nodes are part of the body's disease-fighting immune system. NHL is one of two types of cancers that cluster there—the other being Hodgkin's disease. Both begin in white blood cells, which begin to grow abnormally in the lymph nodes. NHL is the more aggressive, and more common, variety of the disease. Cancerous white blood cells abandon their disease-fighting role and begin to multiply abnormally. Chemotherapy and radiation are often used to treat the disease. Sometimes, biological therapy, marshaling the body's immune system to attack the cancerous cells, can help.

The National Cancer Institute (NCI) is one of the twenty-seven institutes and centers that comprise the U.S. National Institutes of Health, an agency of the U.S. Department of Health and Human Services. The NCI was established by act of Congress in 1937. It supports and coordinates cancer research and education.

Non-Hodgkin's lymphoma (also called NHL) is cancer that begins in the lymphatic system. To understand this disease, it is helpful to know about the lymphatic system.

The lymphatic system is part of the body's immune system. The immune system fights infections and other diseases.

In the lymphatic system, a network of lymph vessels carries clear fluid called lymph. Lymph vessels lead to small, round organs called lymph nodes. Lymph nodes are filled

National Cancer Institute, "What You Need to Know About Non-Hodgkin's Lymphoma," NIH Publication No. 05–1567, 2002. Reproduced by permission.

with lymphocytes (a type of white blood cell). The lymph nodes trap and remove bacteria or other harmful substances that may be in the lymph. Groups of lymph nodes are found in the neck, underarms, chest, abdomen, and groin.

Other parts of the lymphatic system include the tonsils, spleen, and thymus. Lymphatic tissue is also found in other parts of the body including the stomach, skin, and small intestine.

How NHL Begins

There are many types of non-Hodgkin's lymphoma. All types of lymphoma begin in cells of the lymphatic system. Normally, cells grow and divide to form new cells as the body needs them. When cells grow old, they die, and new cells take their place. Sometimes this process goes wrong. New cells form when the body does not need them, and old cells do not die when they should. These extra cells can form a mass of tissue called a growth or tumor.

Non-Hodgkin's lymphoma begins when a lymphocyte (a B cell or T cell) becomes abnormal. Usually, non-Hodgkin's lymphoma starts in a B cell in a lymph node. The abnormal cell divides to make copies of itself. The new cells divide again and again, making more and more abnormal cells. The abnormal cells are cancer cells. They do not die when they should. They do not protect the body from infections or other diseases. Also, the cancer cells can spread to nearly any other part of the body.

Risk factors

Doctors can seldom explain why one person develops non-Hodgkin's lymphoma and another does not. But research shows that certain risk factors increase the chance that a person will develop this disease. In general, the risk factors for non-Hodgkin's lymphoma include the following:

- Weak immune system: Having a weak immune system (from an inherited condition, HIV infection, or certain drugs) increases the risk of developing non-Hodgkin's lymphoma.

- Certain infections: Having certain types of infections increases the risk of developing lymphoma. However, lymphoma is not contagious. You cannot "catch" lymphoma from another person. The following are the main types of infection that can increase the risk of lymphoma:

- Human immunodeficiency virus (HIV): HIV is the virus that causes AIDS. People who have HIV infection are at much greater risk of some types of non-Hodgkin's lymphoma.

- Epstein-Barr virus (EBV): Infection with EBV has been linked to an increased risk of lymphoma. In Africa, EBV infection is linked to Burkitt's lymphoma.

- Helicobacter pylori: H. pylori are bacteria that can cause stomach ulcers. They also increase a person's risk of lymphoma in the stomach lining.

- Human T-cell leukemia/lymphoma (HTLV-1): Infection with HTLV-1 increases a person's risk of lymphoma and leukemia.

- Hepatitis C virus: Some studies have found an increased risk of lymphoma in people with hepatitis C virus. More research is needed to understand the role of hepatitis C virus.

- Age: Although non-Hodgkin's lymphoma can occur in young people, the chance of developing this disease goes up with age. Most people with non-Hodgkin's lymphoma are older than 60. . . .

Symptoms

Non-Hodgkin's lymphoma can cause many symptoms:

- Swollen, painless lymph nodes in the neck, armpits, or groin

- Unexplained weight loss

- Fever

- Soaking night sweats

- Coughing, trouble breathing, or chest pain

- Weakness and tiredness that don't go away

- Pain, swelling, or a feeling of fullness in the abdomen

Most often, these symptoms are not due to cancer. Infections or other health problems may also cause these symptoms. Anyone with symptoms that do not go away within 2 weeks should see a doctor so that problems can be diagnosed and treated.

Diagnosis

If you have swollen lymph nodes or other symptoms that suggest non-Hodgkin's lymphoma, your doctor will help you find out whether they are from cancer or some other cause. Your doctor may ask about your personal and family medical history.

You may have some of the following exams and tests:

- Physical exam: Your doctor checks for swollen lymph nodes in your neck, underarms, and groin. Your doctor also checks your spleen and liver to see if they are swollen.

- Blood tests: The lab does a complete blood count to check the number of blood cells. The lab also checks for other substances, such as lactate dehydrogenase (LDH). Lymphoma may cause a high level of LDH.

- Chest x-rays: You may have x-rays to check for swollen lymph nodes or other signs of disease in your chest.

- Biopsy: Your doctor removes tissue to look for lymphoma cells. A biopsy is the only sure way to diagnose lymphoma. Your doctor may remove an entire lymph node (excisional biopsy) or only part of a lymph node (incisional biopsy). A pathologist checks the tissue for lymphoma cells with a microscope. . . .

Your doctor needs to know the extent (stage) of non-Hodgkin's lymphoma to plan the best treatment. . . .

The stages of non-Hodgkin's lymphoma are as follows:

- Stage I: The lymphoma cells are in a single lymph node group (such as in the neck or underarm). Or, if the abnormal cells are not in the lymph nodes, they are in only one part of a tissue or organ (such as the lung, but not the liver or bone marrow).

- Stage II: The lymphoma cells are in at least two lymph node groups on the same side of (either above or below) the diaphragm. Or, the lymphoma cells are in an organ and the lymph nodes near that organ (on the same side of the diaphragm). There may be lymphoma cells in other lymph node groups on the same side of the diaphragm.

- Stage III: The lymphoma is in groups of lymph nodes above and below the diaphragm. It also may be found in an organ or tissue near these lymph node groups.

- Stage IV: The lymphoma is throughout at least one organ or tissue (in addition to the lymph nodes). Or, it is in the liver, blood, or bone marrow. . . .

Different Treatments for Different Stages

If you have indolent [slow-growing] non-Hodgkin's lymphoma without symptoms, you may not need treatment for the cancer right away. The doctor watches your health closely so that treatment can start when you begin to have symptoms. Not getting cancer treatment right away is called watchful waiting.

If you have indolent lymphoma with symptoms, you will probably receive chemotherapy and biological therapy. Radiation therapy may be used for patients with Stage I or Stage II lymphoma.

If you have aggressive lymphoma, the treatment is usually chemotherapy and biological therapy. Radiation therapy also may be used.

If non-Hodgkin's lymphoma comes back after treatment, doctors call this a relapse or recurrence. People whose lymphoma comes back after treatment may receive stem cell transplantation.

Because cancer treatments often harm healthy cells and tissues, side effects are common. Side effects depend mainly on the type and extent of the treatment. Side effects may not be the same for each person, and they may change from one treatment session to the next. The younger a person is, the easier it may be to cope with treatment and its side effects.

Before treatment starts, the health care team will explain possible side effects and suggest ways to help you manage them. . . .

At any stage of the disease, you can have treatments to control pain and other symptoms, to relieve the side effects of therapy, and to ease emotional and practical problems. This kind of treatment is called supportive care. . . .

The Promise of Cancer Research

Scientists are searching for causes of non-Hodgkin's lymphoma. Also, doctors all over the country are studying new ways to treat lymphoma. Clinical trials (research studies in which people volunteer to take part) find out whether promising approaches to treatment are safe and effective. Research already has led to advances.

Researchers are studying many types of treatments for lymphoma:

- Chemotherapy: Doctors are testing new drugs that kill cancer cells. They are working with many drugs and drug combinations. They also are looking at ways of combining drugs with other treatments, such as biological therapy.

- Radiation therapy: Doctors are testing radiation treatment alone and with chemotherapy.

- Biological therapy: New types of biological therapy are under study. For example, researchers are making cancer vaccines that may help the immune system kill lymphoma cells. Also, doctors are studying a type of biological therapy that delivers radiation directly to cancer cells.

- Stem cell transplantation: Doctors are studying stem cell transplantation in people with newly diagnosed lymphoma and those who have already been treated.

People who join clinical trials may be among the first to benefit if a new approach is effective. And even if participants do not benefit directly, they still help doctors learn more about the disease and how to control it. Although clinical trials may pose some risks, researchers do all they can to protect their patients.

CHAPTER 2

Cancer Treatments

Chemotherapy

Toni Rizzo and Rhonda Cloos, RN

One of the most common ways to treat cancer is with chemotherapy, a treatment that aims to kill cancer cells. In the following selection authors Toni Rizzo and Rhonda Cloos, RN, explain the various types of chemotherapy and the ways in which chemo is given to patients. While there are multiple side effects that can be associated with chemotherapy, such as nausea and hair loss, Rizzo and Cloos also acknowledge the benefits that can be gained from the treatment, such as complete remission of the cancer. Toni Rizzo has undergraduate degrees in biology and education, as well as training and certification as a cytologist (specialist in cancer cellular diagnosis), and an MS degree in communication. Rhonda Cloos is an author and registered nurse.

The main purpose of chemotherapy is to kill cancer cells. It can be used as the primary form of treatment or as a supplement to other treatments. Chemotherapy is often used to treat patients with cancer that has spread from the place in the body where it started (metastasized), but it may also be used to keep cancer from coming back (adjuvant therapy). Chemotherapy destroys cancer cells anywhere in the body. It even kills cells that have broken off from the main tumor and traveled through the blood or lymph systems to other parts of the body. Chemotherapy can cure some types of cancer. In some cases, it is used to slow the growth of cancer cells or to keep the cancer from spreading to other parts of the body. When a cancer has been removed by surgery, chemotherapy may be used to keep the cancer from coming back (adjuvant therapy). It is also helpful in reducing the tumor size prior to surgery (primary [neoadjuvant] chemotherapy). Chemo-

Toni Rizzo and Rhonda Cloos, RN, "Chemotherapy." *The Gale Encyclopedia of Cancer: A Guide to Cancer and Its Treatments,* Second Edition. Jacqueline L. Longe, Editor. Farmington Hills, MI: Thomson Gale, 2005.

therapy can ease the symptoms of cancer (palliate), helping some patients have a better quality of life.

Adjuvant Chemotherapy

Adjuvant chemotherapy refers to giving patients anticancer drugs after the primary tumor has been removed and there is no evidence that cancer remains in the body. It was first studied in the 1950s. This form of treatment initially gained popularity because it showed promise in improving the survival for patients with certain cancers. The theory was that adjuvant chemotherapy would attack microscopic cancer cells that remained after tumor removal. Adjuvant chemotherapy may be effective in some types of cancers, including breast cancer, colorectal cancer, osteogenic sarcoma, and Wilms' tumor.

A patient's response to adjuvant therapy is determined by a variety of factors, including drug dosage, schedule of drug therapy, and drug resistance. Toxic side effects and cost-effectiveness are other important issues. This area is undergoing further investigation.

Primary (Neoadjuvant) Chemotherapy

Primary chemotherapy, also sometimes called neoadjuvant chemotherapy or induction chemotherapy, is the use of anticancer drugs as the main form of treatment. Chemotherapy can be the primary treatment with cancers such as these: certain lymphomas, childhood and some adult forms of Hodgkin's disease, Wilms' tumor, embryonal rhabdomyosarcoma, and small cell lung cancer.

Primary chemotherapy can also be used to treat tumors prior to surgery or radiation. In some cases, the tumor may be so large that surgery to remove it would destroy major organs or would be quite disfiguring. Primary neoadjuvant chemotherapy may reduce the tumor size, making it possible for a surgeon to perform a less traumatic operation. Examples of cancers in which primary chemotherapy may be followed-up with less extensive surgeries include: anal cancer, bladder cancer, breast cancer, esophageal cancer, laryngeal cancer, osteogenic sarcoma, and soft tissue sarcoma.

An advantage of primary chemotherapy is that the blood vessels are intact since they have not been exposed to surgery or radiation. Therefore, drugs can easily travel through the bloodstream toward the tumor. In fact, the therapy can improve the tumor's blood flow, making it more receptive to the impact of radiation. In addition, the use of chemotherapy before surgical removal of cancer allows the physician to assess the responsiveness of the tumor to the drug(s) used. Since not all chemotherapy regimens are equally effective, knowing how a particular tumor responds to the chemotherapy regimen prescribed can be an advantage in treating the disease.

Primary chemotherapy does have drawbacks. Some cancer cells may be drug-resistant, making the therapy ineffective. (Although discovering that the drug is ineffective minimizes the number of cycles of the drug that the patient must undergo.) The drug may not significantly reduce tumor size, or the tumor may continue to grow despite treatment. Furthermore, the initial use of a drug may lead to higher toxicity when chemotherapy is given later in the course of treatment.

Primary chemotherapy is becoming the norm in treating some patients with certain cancers, such as specific types of lymphomas, some small cell lung cancers, childhood cancers, head and neck cancers, and locally advanced breast cancer. Additional research using this type of chemotherapy is underway.

Combination Chemotherapy

In most cases, single anticancer drugs cannot cure cancer alone. The use of two or more drugs together is often a more effective alternative. This approach is called combination chemotherapy. Scientific studies of different drug combinations help doctors learn which combinations work best for various types of cancers.

Combination chemotherapy provides a higher chance of destroying cancerous cells. An oncologist decides which chemotherapy drug or combination of drugs will work best for each patient. Different drugs attack cancer cells at varying stages of their growth cycles, making the combination a stronger weapon against cancerous cells. Furthermore, using a combination of drugs may reduce the chance of drug resistance.

When selecting the combination of drugs, a variety of factors are examined. It is important for each drug to be effective against the particular tumor being targeted. Toxicity must also be studied to be sure that each different drug used in a combination is not toxic for the same organ. For example, if two drugs are each toxic to the liver, the combination could be more damaging to that organ.

How Chemotherapy Is Given

Chemotherapy medications enter a person's body in different ways, depending on the drugs to be given and the type of cancer.

The goal is for the chemotherapy drug to reach the tumor. Some areas of the body are less accessible for anticancer drugs, and this is considered when the doctor determines the route of administration. For example, the blood-brain barrier refers to the inability of some anticancer drugs to travel through the bloodstream and enter the brain or the fluid surrounding the brain. Areas of the body that are inaccessible to a particular drug create a phenomenon called the sanctuary effect. In other words, the tumor is safe because the chemotherapy cannot reach it. To overcome a problem such as this one, the doctor must consider the route that will most effectively deliver the drug to the cancerous cells. Chemotherapy may be given by one or more of the following methods:

- oral (by mouth)

- injection (intramuscular or subcutaneous)

- intravenous (IV)

- intra-arterial (into the arteries)

- intralesional (directly into the tumor)

- intraperitoneal (into the peritoneal cavity)

- intrathecal (into the spinal fluid)

- topically (applied to the skin)

Oral, Injection, Intravenous, and Intra-Arterial Methods

Oral chemotherapy is given by mouth in the form of a pill, capsule, or liquid. This is the easiest method and can usually be done at home.

Intramuscular (IM) chemotherapy is injected into a muscle. Chemotherapy given by intramuscular injection is absorbed into the blood more slowly than IV chemotherapy. Because of this, the effects of IM chemotherapy may last longer than chemotherapy given intravenously. Chemotherapy may also be injected subcutaneously (SQ or SC), which means under the skin.

Intravenous (IV) chemotherapy is the most common way to deliver anticancer drugs into a person's body. The drug is injected directly into a vein. A small needle is inserted into a vein on the hand or lower arm.

Chemotherapy may also be given by a catheter or port inserted into a central vein or body cavity, where it can remain for an extended period of time. A port is a small reservoir or container that is placed in a vein or under the skin in the area where the drug will be given. These methods eliminate the need for repeated injections and may allow patients to spend less time in the hospital while receiving chemotherapy. A common location for a permanent catheter is the external jugular vein in the neck. Catheters and ports require meticulous care and cleaning to avoid complications, such as blood clots or infection. They may be inserted using a surgical procedure.

Chemotherapy given by the IV method may be administered intermittently or continuously. The main reasons for a continuous flow are to increase effectiveness against the tumor or to lower toxicity. Some drugs perform more effectively when exposed to the cancer over a period of time, making a continuous flow more desirable. A drug that is commonly used to treat colorectal cancer in continuous infusions is 5-fluorouracil, also known as 5-FU or fluorouracil. A drug that has less toxicity to the heart with continued infusion is doxorubicin, also known as Adriamycin. In some cases, toxicity occurs when the drug reaches a peak level. Offering a continuous infusion prevents the drug from reaching this level, thus lowering the chance of toxic side effects.

Cancerous tumors require a supply of blood and oxygen so that they can grow. They get these essentials from the arteries that supply organs with their blood and oxygen. Putting chemotherapy drugs into the arteries provides good access to the cancerous tumor. Intra-arterial chemotherapy is not designed for all patients. The tumor must be confined to one specific organ and the blood supply to the tumor must be accessible. The liver is the most common organ targeted in this type of chemotherapy, although it is also effective in certain brain cancers. Its use in head and neck cancers remains controversial. Further use of this type of chemotherapy is being investigated.

A catheter is inserted using radiologic techniques or surgery. Surgical insertion is the most common. Although it is less costly and less stressful, radiologic insertion results in a catheter that cannot stay in place as long as one inserted surgically. A radiologically inserted catheter stays in place for weeks compared to surgically inserted catheters designed to stay in place from weeks to years. In the long run, the surgically implanted arterial catheter has fewer complications, such as thrombosis or infection, and is more highly acceptable to the patient.

The radiologically placed catheter is initially inserted into an artery in the person's arm or leg, and then it is guided to its final destination near the tumor, where it can remain for an extended period.

The catheters require meticulous care to keep them clean and securely in place, which lessen the chance of complications. Problems associated with catheters include movement of the tip, blood clots and infection.

Pumps may be used to move the drug through the artery and into the tumor. A pump may be external or internally planted. External pumps range from large machines found in hospitals to portable wallet-sized devices. Implanted pumps give patients greater freedom, and are safe and effective. Some internal pumps deliver a constant flow of drugs, while others are programmed to deliver intermittent doses.

Drugs used for intra-arterial chemotherapy include FUDR (floxuridine), fluorouracil, mitomycin, cisplatin, and streptomycin. Less frequently, doxorubicin has been used intra-arterially for treating certain cancers of the breast, bladder, stomach, and other areas.

Intralesional, Intraperitoneal, Intrathecal, and Topical Methods

Intralesional chemotherapy is the injection of anticancer drugs directly into a tumor that is in the skin, under the skin, or in an organ inside the body. Some examples involving the use of intralesional chemotherapy include melanoma and Kaposi's sarcoma. This type of chemotherapy shows promise for other malignancies such as laryngeal cancers, and further uses are under investigation.

Intraperitoneal (IP) chemotherapy is administered into the abdominal cavity through a catheter or port that is put into place by surgery.

Ovarian cancer is sometimes treated with IP chemotherapy because this type of cancer usually stays within a confined area. This type of therapy is only suitable for some patients. Ovarian cancer patients whose tumors have a diameter greater than two centimeters may not receive this therapy because the anticancer drug does not reach very far into the tumor. Also, patients whose cancers are resistant to certain drugs may not undergo IP therapy. Patients with smaller tumors, or those who show response to chemotherapy are better candidates.

Drugs used in IP chemotherapy include cisplatin, paclitaxel, floxuridine, 5-FU, mitoxantrone, carboplatin, and alfa-interferon.

Intrathecal chemotherapy is the injection of anticancer drugs into the spinal fluid. This method is used primarily in treating acute lymphocytic leukemia. It is effective in placing the anticancer drug directly into the cerebrospinal fluid that surrounds the spinal cord and the brain. A spinal tap, also called lumbar puncture, is the procedure usually used to gain access to the spinal fluid. If many treatments are needed, a device called an Ommaya reservoir may be used. This device is inserted under the scalp and allows injection of anticancer drugs throughout the spinal fluid via the reservoir. Patients can go home with the Ommaya reservoir in place. Common drugs used intrathecally include methotrexate and cytarabine, which are usually given by a doctor with a nurse's assistance. Some leukemia patients receive IV treatments at the same time they are having intrathecal treatments.

Topical chemotherapy is given as a cream or ointment applied directly to the cancer. This method is more common in the treatment of certain types of skin cancer. An example is fluorouracil, also known as 5-FU, which is a topical anticancer cream. . . .

Risks of Chemotherapy

Chemotherapy drugs are toxic to normal cells as well as cancer cells. A dose that will destroy cancer cells will probably cause damage to some normal cells. Doctors adjust doses to do the least amount of harm possible to normal cells. Some patients feel few or no side effects, and others may have more serious side effects. In some cases, a dose adjustment is all that is needed to reduce or stop a side effect.

A person may experience a side effect right away or the reaction may be delayed. Side effects are classified as follows:

- acute, develops within 24 hours of treatment

- delayed, develops after 24 hours but within sex to eight weeks of treatment

- short-term, combination of acute and delayed

- late/long-term, develops months or years after treatment, or lasts for an extended period of time

- expected, a side effect that develops in three quarters of patients

- common, occurs in 25-75% of patients

- uncommon/occasional, occurs in less than a quarter of patients

- rare, occurs in 5% of patients

- very rare, occurs in less than 1% of patients

Certain chemotherapy drugs have more side effects than others. While some drugs have immediate effects, other effects are delayed. Patients are encouraged to discuss the potential for side effects with their doctor. They must seek immediate medical attention if they are experiencing any unusual symptoms. Some of the most common side effects are discussed in this section.

Possible Side Effects of Chemotherapy

Nausea and vomiting are common, but can usually be controlled by taking antinausea drugs, drinking enough fluids, and avoiding spicy foods. Loss of appetite (anorexia) may be due to nausea or the stress of undergoing cancer treatment. Drugs that have a high likelihood of causing nausea or vomiting include cisplatin, mechlorethamine, streptozocin, dacarbazine, carmustine, and dactinomycin. Those with moderate nausea-inducing potential include cyclophosphamide, doxorubicin, carboplatin, mitomycin, and L-asparaginase. Anticancer drugs with a low chance of causing nausea or vomiting include fluorouracil, methotrexate, etoposide, vincristine, and bleomycin.

Some chemotherapy drugs cause hair loss, but it is almost always temporary. Hair re-growth may not begin until several weeks have passed since the final treatment. This is the most common impact that chemotherapy has on the outer surfaces of the body. In some patients, an ice wrap, called an ice turban, can reduce hair loss. The effectiveness will depend on factors such as the type of drug, dose, and treatment schedule. This preventive treatment must be avoided by patients with leukemia, lymphoma, mycosis fungoides or by those with scalp tumors. People should use with caution if they have conditions such as vasculitis, cryoglobulinemia or a history of radiation to the head. Patients should discuss the ice turban treatment with their doctor before trying it.

Low blood cell counts caused by the effect of chemotherapy on the bone marrow can lead to anemia, infections, and easy bleeding and bruising. Patients with anemia have too few red blood cells to deliver oxygen and nutrients to the body's tissues. Anemic patients feel tired and weak. If red blood cell levels fall too low, a blood transfusion may be given.

Patients receiving chemotherapy are more likely to get infections. This happens because their infection-fighting white blood cells are reduced. The level of reduction can vary depending on the dose and schedule of treatments, and whether the drug is used alone or in combination with other anticancer agents.

It is important for chemotherapy patients to avoid infection. When the white blood cell count drops too low, the doctor may prescribe medications called colony stimulating factors that help white blood cells grow. Neupogen and Leukine are two colony stimulants used as treatments to help fight infection.

Platelets are blood cells that make the blood clot. When patients do not have enough platelets, they may bleed or bruise easily, even from small injuries. Patients with low blood platelets should take precautions to avoid injuries. Medicines such as aspirin and other pain relievers can affect platelets and slow down the clotting process.

Chemotherapy can cause irritation and dryness in the mouth and throat. An inflammation in the mouth is called stomatitis. Painful sores may form that can bleed and become infected. Precautions to avoid this side effect include getting dental care before chemotherapy begins, brushing the teeth and gums regularly with a soft brush, and avoiding mouth washes that contain salt or alcohol. Good oral hygiene is important. It is helpful for some patients to chew on ice chips for half an hour during chemotherapy treatments, but this should be discussed with the doctor before it is done.

More Possible Side Effects

Cancer patients may develop neurological problems due to the cancer or the anticancer drugs. A variety of problems can develop, including altered mental alertness, changes in taste and smell, seizures, and peripheral neuropathy (tingling and burning sensations and/or weakness or numbness in the hands and/or feet). Different drugs can lead to different types of neurological disorders. Patients should discuss neurological symptoms with the doctor.

Some anticancer drugs are damaging to the heart. In these cases, the dosage is closely monitored in an attempt to avoid heart damage. Specific drugs that may be toxic to the heart include doxorubicin, daunorubicin, high doses of cyclophosphamide, and, in some cases, 5-FU. Patients experiencing chest pain or any cardiac symptoms should seek immediate medical help.

A number of anticancer drugs can damage the kidney. Examples include high doses of methotrexate or 6-MP, as well as regular doses of L-asparaginase, cisplatin, mithramycin, streptozocin, and mitomycin C. Some kidney problems can be lessened by taking in adequate amounts of fluids. A secondary danger of kidney damage is that a less functional kidney can be more susceptible to further toxicity caused by other anticancer drugs that the patient is taking.

Cancer patients who have had radiation in the chest area are more susceptible to respiratory complications. Nitrosourea or bleomycin cause the most common type of respiratory toxicity, called pulmonary fibrosis. Patients should get immediate medical assistance if they have difficulty breathing.

Some drugs can lead to impaired sexual function. Alkylating agents and procarbazine may result in the absence of sperm in a man and the lack of menstruation in a woman. Patients of child-bearing age are usually told to refrain from conceiving while undergoing chemotherapy because of the defects it can cause in the fetus.

Some anticancer drugs can impact a person's vision. High doses of cyclophosphamide can cause blurred vision in children, while some alkylating agents can cause cataracts. Tamoxifen may be damaging to the retina, and cisplatin can damage the optic nerve. Conjunctivitis, commonly called pinkeye, is a treatable problem that occurs with many anticancer drugs.

Results of Chemotherapy

The main goal of chemotherapy is to cure cancer. Many cancers are cured by chemotherapy. The chemotherapy treatment may be used in combination with surgery to keep a cancer from spreading to other parts of the body. Some widespread, fast-growing cancers are more difficult to treat. In these cases, chemotherapy may slow the growth of the cancer cells.

Doctors can tell if the chemotherapy is working by the results of medical tests. Physical examination, blood tests, and X rays are all used to check the effects of treatment on the cancer.

The possible outcomes of chemotherapy are:

- Complete remission or response. The cancer completely disappears for at least one month. The course of chemotherapy is completed and the patient is tested regularly for a recurrence.

- Partial response. The cancer shrinks in size by at least 30-50%, the reduction in size is maintained for at least one month, and no new lesions are found during treatment. The same chemotherapy may be continued or a different combination of drugs may be used.

- Minor response. The cancer shrinks 1-29%.

- Stabilization. The cancer does not grow or shrink. Other therapy options may be explored. A tumor may stay stabilized for many years.

- Progressive disease. The cancer continues to increase in size by at least 25%, or new lesions are noted. Other therapy options may be explored.

- A secondary malignancy may develop from the one being treated, and that second cancer may need additional chemotherapy or other treatment.

Radiation Therapy

Michelangelo Delfino and Mary E. Day

In the following selection Michelangelo Delfino and Mary E. Day, two experts in radiation therapy, explain the various radiation techniques for the treatment of cancer. Radiation is helpful if it kills tumor cells without damaging too many healthy cells. To accomplish this doctors try to focus beams of radiation on the tumors. Different kinds of radiation are harnessed for different approaches. In some cases, doctors place a radiation source as close as possible to the tumor. In others, they try to get the immune system to carry radioactive atoms into the tumor cells.

Michelangelo Delfino and Mary E. Day are former employees of Varian Medical Systems Inc., a leading supplier of radiation oncology products. They are the inventors of radiation health care products and authors of dozens of scientific publications.

The idea of using deadly ionizing radiation as therapy is a bit of an oxymoron. High-dose radiation certainly does not heal and nor does it selectively kill only malignant cells—it kills all cells or at least disrupts the DNA in all cells that it contacts. In that sense, it is really no different than a surgeon's knife. Being bloodless makes it seem the much more friendlier killer.

The therapeutic value of radiation rests in its presumed ability to destroy a significantly greater number of bad cells than good ones, and not encourage any healthy cells to later become cancerous cells. The goal of treatment is to remove permanently all the cancer. Surgery is by far the most common method of treating cancer, and radiation is one highly sought after alternative.

Various high-energy X-ray and gamma ray sources are used to treat cancer. Artificially produced X-rays are far and away the most frequently used form of radiation today and the technology for producing them is well developed. High-energy X-ray beams are mostly created using a linear accelerator, also called a linac. These rather large machines first produce very high-energy electrons that on passing through a thin tungsten target generate a beam of X-rays that are capable of penetrating human tissue to a depth of at least 6 inches thereby affecting ionization [the alteration of atoms into ions by radiation] in any cell in the body.

In 1953, an 8 million volt (MV) linac was first used to treat English cancer patients in the U.K. Today, medical linacs operate from 5 MV to greater than 25 MV and are the workhorse of most modern cancer radiotherapy equipment collectively referred to as external beam radiation therapy (EBRT). Nothing else can so reliably deliver a deeply penetrating and deadly beam of radiation as linac based EBRT.

Widely Used System

"We live and die by radiation therapy," touts the world's leading manufacturer of integrated cancer therapy systems with a near 60% of the world's oncology radiation market (Varian Medical Systems). Indeed, the Palo Alto, California based corporation has a near monopoly on radiotherapy equipment having sold more than 3500 linac based EBRT systems used to treat more than 1 million patients per year and over 50% of all cancer patients in the United States alone.

The Varian machines are extremely robust and dependable and have the advantage of producing a high energy X-ray beam only when the machine is turned on. As with most anything that is exposed to radiation, the irradiated parts of the machine become mildly radioactive thereby requiring safety and disposal considerations.

Instead of a machine with moving parts, a radioisotope alone can be used for radiotherapy. Cobalt-60, a gamma radiation source with a half-life of 5.27 years was first used in the U.K. by the London Regional Cancer Centre to treat cancer in 1951. The treatment was simple—expose the patient and the tumor to the stationary radiation source and let the deadly dual 1.17 and 1.33 MeV beam irradiate its human target.

The downside of these cobalt-60 machines is that the radiation source is always "turned on" and several inches of lead are required to protect everyone else from exposure (e.g., 2 inches of lead absorb 95% of a 1.5 MeV gamma ray beam). . . .

Gamma Ray Knife

Today, MDS Nordion, the 8000 plus employee "global leader in radioisotope technology" with its main facility in Ottawa, Canada supplies more than 80% of the world's need for cobalt-60. The present day's version of the original cobalt-60 shuttered lead box is called a Gamma Knife, a far more sophisticated tool that features 201 digitally-focused gamma ray beams capable of delivering precise tumor targeting. This tool was invented in Sweden in 1968 by Lars Leksell a physician and is often referred to as the Leksell Gamma Knife in his honor.

Like a surgeon's scalpel, the radiation beam is imperfect in limiting its cutting edge to just the tumor. One of the major problems with EBRT is its inability to confine the lethal radiation to the malignancy so to avoid destroying healthy tissue. This problem is exacerbated [worsened] in practice as the patient breathes and moves while being irradiated. Surprising no parent for sure, . . . workers report from the Duke University Medical Center that more than 93% of all children 2 years and younger require anesthesia during the most mundane radiation treatment to keep them immobile.

Computer Aided Targeting

Intensity modulated radiation therapy (IMRT) uses highly sophisticated computer programs to *a priori* [preselected] shape the radiation beam using a dynamic computer model of the tumor. The idea here is to minimize the ratio of normal tissue dose to tumor dose. Conformality and pencil-tip accuracy of the radiation and at an elevated radiation dose are achieved. But to be truly effective, IMRT requires real time anatomical mapping of the target area during treatment to account for tumor movement, losses in tumor volume, and changes in the shape of the tumor. None of this can be modeled in real time with a computer and the medical practitioner must rely on such modeling to estimate the tumor's true location.

Associated Risks

And while the University of Chicago's Department of Radiation and Cellular Oncology suggests that IMRT is more useful to academic research than to patient therapy there are other issues. [Eric J.] Hall and [Li-Jun] Wu of the Columbia University College of Physicians and Surgeons and others point out that the very nature of IMRT necessitates a longer radiation time, a larger volume of non-malignant tissue exposed to radiation, and an increase in total exposure—all of which nearly double the risk of radiation-induced secondary cancers with post-exposure lifetime. . . .

Aside from these drawbacks, the University of Wisconsin, Madison determined other reasons why only 10% of all radiotherapy patients actually benefit from IMRT. First, half of all patients who undergo radiotherapy are treated solely for palliation—pain relief—and palliation rarely requires pinpoint accuracy. Second, only 20% of the patients who do benefit— primarily those with tumors of the head, neck, and prostate— require IMRT's accuracy. . . .

Stereotactic Radiosurgery

Seventeen years before the Gamma Knife, Lars Leksell, invented the concept of radiosurgery—a one-session radiation therapy. Radiosurgery uses precisely guided radiation from a linac or a Gamma Knife to destroy tumors. It is not surgery *per se* but a physically noninvasive treatment that requires no incision. Unlike traditional surgery, radiosurgery is not associated with complications due to infection, anesthesia side effects, facial weakness, hearing loss, and brain stem injury. When radiosurgery is coupled with stereotactic placement in which the head and neck are physically fixed during treatment via a three-dimensional skeletal positioning device, the accuracy of radiosurgery is improved and higher doses are realized.

According to American Shared Hospital Services (AMS), a 12-person publicly traded company based in San Francisco providing Gamma Knife support to hospitals in the United States there are approximately 103 Gamma Knife centers in the United States and 234 units installed worldwide as of 2006. AMS claims that each center treats on average 175 patients annually. Elekta, Inc., the company that manufactures the Gamma Knife, reported in 2006 that more than 350,000 patients had been treated in more than 220 hospitals worldwide with their product.

Dealing with Resistance

It is well established that tumor cells that have become hypoxic or oxygen deficient are the most resistant to radiation, requiring up to a three times higher radiation dose to destroy. These cancers are so resistant in fact that cancer patients with hypoxic tumors are sometimes asked to breathe a gas mixture containing less than half the oxygen by volume in air while being irradiated.

The air we breathe is normally 78% nitrogen, 21% oxygen, and less than 1% other gases—argon and carbon dioxide—by volume. In hypoxic radiotherapy, the use of air with less oxygen momentarily renders nearby healthy tissue just as radiation resistant as the hypoxic tumor which then increases the selectivity of destroying malignant tumors over healthy tissue. Alternatively, in hyperbaric radiotherapy, the patient is placed in a chamber with 100% oxygen at greater than one atmospheric pressure while being treated. This technique has been used in Europe by a working oncology group and reported as improving overall survival and local tumor control in head and neck cancers as well as in managing radiation-induced complications after irradiation.

Hypoxic modifying drugs are also employed in combination with radiotherapy to improve tumor selectivity. Cisplatin, an organic-platinum compound approved for use in the United States by the Food and Drug Administration in 1978 for chemotherapy, is an example of a radiosensitizer—a drug that under certain conditions makes a cancer cell more sensitive to the effects of ionizing radiation.

Radioactive Implants

Brachytherapy is a form of radiotherapy in which the radiation source is placed in direct contact with the cancer. This concept of internal radiotherapy was apparently first suggested in 1903 by Alexander Graham Bell—the inventor of the telephone—using naturally occurring radium.

One of brachytherapy's earliest patients was the remarkable [opera composer] Giacomo Puccini. In 1924, this perennial smoker of cigars was diagnosed with an incurable form of cancer of the larynx (voice box) and treated with both internal and external radium brachytherapy. Within 4 days of treatment Puccini's heart failed and the world lost the last great composer of opera.

A wide variety of radioisotopes for use in brachytherapy are artificially produced in both nuclear reactors and in cyclotrons. The Oak Ridge National Laboratory in Tennessee is a major source of reactor fission products in the United States. Smaller nuclear reactors are also used throughout the world to produce specific isotopes. Cyclotrons are more costly to operate than reactors but they have the advantage of producing radioisotopes with higher specific activities (amount of radioactivity per amount of material) and radioisotopes that are free of other radioisotopes. . . .

Inserting a Wire

In high-dose rate (HDR) brachytherapy, a wire tipped with a gamma-emitting radioisotope is inserted in a catheter (a slender flexible tube) that has been placed inside a tumor (called an interstitial implant procedure) or near a tumor. The radioactive source is positioned in the tumor for a relatively short period of time. This treatment has been applied to cancers of the prostate, esophagus, lung, and breast, among others. Intracavity brachytherapy, for example, is used to treat cervical and vaginal cancers by temporarily holding a radioactive source inside the vagina. . . .

Alternatively, in early stages of prostate cancer, dozens of lower-dose radioactive seeds—metal encased radioisotopes the size of a grain of rice—are surgically implanted directly into the tumor to remain and radiate according to their half-life. In both cases, healthy tissue is damaged in so far as to the extent that it is affected by the attenuated radiation source. Radiation dissipates inversely as the distance from the source is squared—tissue twice as far away from the radioactive seed receives 1/4 the dose.

Iodine-125 (60-day half-life) and palladium-103 (17-day half-life) are the two most commonly used radioisotopes in permanent seed implants. These isotopes are a source of 27 keV gamma rays and 21 keV X-rays, respectively and thus afford the clinician relatively easy protection because of their low energy.

Effects on Lifestyle

Radioactive gold-198 (combination gamma plus beta emitter with a 2.7-day half-life) is another attractive seed implant. Gold is chemically inert and so as in dentistry, it finds use in the treatment of tongue cancer, a place in the body where most metals would corrode and ultimately dissolve in the saliva (spit) and plaque bacteria mix. . . .

Permanent seed implants can affect lifestyle. In one case at least, a cancer patient undergoing permanent seed implant treatment was sufficiently radioactive to have set-off an airport security alarm.

More generally, the practice of safe sex, even with a condom, and the sitting of a grandchild on the lap is problematic.

Radioimmunotherapy

Immunotherapy describes treatment that is intended to restore the ability of the body to fight infection. When combined with radiation this treatment is referred to as radioimmunotherapy (RIT). In this method, alpha or beta emitting radioisotope tagged monoclonal antibodies (MAbs)— laboratory synthesized proteins that preferentially attach themselves to tumor cells and signal the body's immune cells to respond favorably—are used to target specific disease sites minimizing toxicity to normal cells.

RIT is expensive, each dose costing several tens of thousands of dollars because of the difficulty of incorporating a radioactive element in a complex organic molecule. . . .

Yttrium-90, a pure 2.28 MeV beta emitter approved for RIT by the FDA [Food and Drug Administration] in February 2002, is safer to use than iodine-131 and lends itself to outpatient (patient goes home the same day) treatment, but does not permit dosimetry [measurement of the body's absorption of radiation]. The dosimetry problem was addressed with some success by a Mayo Clinic researcher who added a gamma emitting indium-111 pretreatment to yttrium-90 RIT experimental cancer trials.

Alpha emitting actinium-225 (10-day half-life) and bismuth-213 (46-min half-life) labeled MAbs are being explored but no alpha radiation sources are as yet FDA approved. Alpha emitters are ideally suited for RIT because they deliver extremely high doses of lethal radiation in cellular distances and present no inordinate handling difficulties. Moreover, because their penetrating range is but a fraction of beta sources toxicity to normal cells is minimal.

Particle Radiation Therapy

In addition to alpha and beta particles, other kinds of subatomic particles can be used to kill cancer cells. Protons, first discovered in 1918 by Ernest Rutherford, the father of nuclear physics, are hydrogen ions positively charged particles that are 1836 times heavier than electrons. In an uncharged atom, the number of protons always equals the number of electrons. Protons if accelerated to a high velocity easily penetrate human tissue and deposit their maximum energy at a depth that is proportional to the accelerating voltage. The maximum energy has a bell-shaped distribution (called a Bragg peak) that can be concentrated in the tumor and so unlike photons that continue to propagate unless annihilated, the collimated or focused proton beam is even more conformal than IMRT. Like high-energy photons, protons ionize atoms and consequently damage DNA. High-energy protons are therapeutically attractive in that they are five times as effective as equivalent energy photons in causing permanent cellular damage.

Proton therapy was first used to treat cancer in 1954. Treatment is not readily accessible, however, because proton therapy facilities cost $100 to $200 million and take several years to build. In fact, there are less than two-dozen proton therapy facilities in the world with no more than 45,000 people treated to date. . . .

Fourteen years after Rutherford's remarkable discovery, James Chadwick in the U.K. identified another deadly radiation product—the neutron. Energetic neutrons are uncharged particles that are slightly heavier than protons and also of therapeutic value because when they quite literally collide with water molecules inside the cell they ionize the surrounding tissue. High-energy neutrons are needed to cause permanent tumor damage and so huge accelerators are required to produce them. The availability of this costly and highly specialized technology is even more limited than proton therapy. There are only three such facilities in the United States, none of which were originally built to treat cancer. Notwithstanding the lack of availability, the Fermilab in Illinois has treated more than 3000 cancer patients since 1976.

Treating Kids with Cancer

Robin M. Lally

You might think that when cancer strikes a child, misery follows. In the following selection, however, Robin M. Lally relates the optimism that many pediatric oncology nurses feel in working with their young patients. They have reason to feel good about their work these days: The survival rate of children with cancer has climbed to nearly 80 percent, Lally reports. However, there are no quick cures. That means nurses have the opportunity to develop deep and positive relationships with the children in their care and their families. Still, more needs to be done to assure kids with cancer have their needs met, according to Lally. Many young cancer patients emerge from their treatment with long-term care needs. Others, unfortunately, will not survive and must have pain relief and psychological support as the premature end of their lives approaches.

Robin M. Lally is a teaching specialist at the University of Minnesota's School of Nursing in Minneapolis.

Karla Wilson, a nurse practitioner at City of Hope National Medical Center in Duarte, CA, began her career in pediatric oncology nursing 31 years ago [1975], when primary care nursing was a new concept. Her desire to provide primary care led her to pediatric oncology, and she never left. Over the years, Wilson says that she learned that "kids with cancer are well kids who just happen to have cancer" and working with them gives nurses the opportunity to provide "hope, realism, and the skills to cope with illness, treatment, survival, and sometimes death," an experience she finds very rewarding.

Wilson's career in pediatric oncology eventually led her to the Association of Pediatric Oncology Nurses (APON), an or-

Robin M. Lally, "Caring for Kids with Cancer Takes Passion, Conviction, and Commitment," *ONS News*, July 2006, p. 1. Republished with permission of publisher, conveyed through Copyright Clearance Center, Inc.

ganization of RNs [registered nurses] caring for children and adolescents with cancer and blood disorders and their families. In 1973, four pediatric oncology nurses founded APON at an impromptu meeting in Atlanta, GA. Today, the organization is more than 2,300 members strong. APON members championed the development of pediatric oncology certification, and, in 1993, 455 nurses took the first Certified Pediatric Oncology Nurse (CPON®) examination, which is now administered by the Oncology Nursing Certification Corporation (ONCC). Wilson served as APON president from 2003–2005....

Rewarding Relationships

"The benefits of getting to know kids and their families far outweigh the bad days," says Dianne Goodrum ..., a staff nurse at St. Jude Affiliate Clinic in Baton Rouge, LA, and coordinator of ONS's [Oncology Nursing Society] Pediatric, Adolescent, and Young Adult Special Interest Group. "I feel lucky to have my job because of the families that have become part of my life."

For all of the nurses interviewed, building long-term relationships with patients and families was a primary reason for practicing pediatric oncology....

Do pediatric nurses ever get depressed by their work? Past ONS President Barbara Britt ..., a nurse care manager in the New Tumors Program at Children's Hospital in Los Angeles, CA, has practiced pediatric oncology nursing for 34 years. "There are sad days, but then there are days that are the highest of highs," she says. One of those highs is when a long-term survivor tracks her down to share a significant event in his or her life, such as a wedding or new baby. "When I started in the field, just about all of my patients eventually died from their disease," she says. "We are in a much different place now."

According to the American Cancer Society, the overall five-year survival for childhood cancer is 79%, although rates are somewhat lower for neuroblastoma (66%) and considerably higher for Wilms tumor and Hodgkin disease (92% and 96%, respectively). Survival of children has improved vastly compared to 30 years ago, when "only little more than half of all children with cancer survived five years or more." Only during the last 60 years has the specialty of pediatric oncology emerged, followed by the emergence of pediatric nurse practitioners and master's degrees in the 1970s and 1980s.

More Cures

"Kids are being cured in record numbers," Britt says. "I have lived through a phase of change in the language we use to describe childhood cancer, from terminal illness to chronic illness with periods of remission and curative potential." Survival, in large part, has been a result of the availability of effective chemotherapy.

"Despite the enormous funding disparity between pediatric oncology research and that for adults, pediatric scientists have been very effective in moving treatment protocols forward," [staff development specialist Janice] Nuuhiwa says. The introduction of targeted therapies in treating children is a recent change that she is happy to see. Approximately 20 targeted agents, such as bevacizumab, gefitinib, and rituximab, are being tested against childhood cancers.

[Clinical nurse specialist Casey] Hooke says the fact that pediatric oncology is a research-based specialty is not only what has kept her in practice but also a reason she is pursuing a doctorate degree. However, she also identities lack of research funding as a deterrent to the development of new treatments. . . .

Care Beyond Survival

Everyone hopes that the survival statistics for children with cancer will continue to improve, but, as Wilson states, "Cure is not enough." Along with increased survival come new challenges.

"We have a whole new generation of Americans—childhood cancer survivors—who come into the healthcare system with their own unique needs," Nuuhiwa says. Britt feels that "survivorship and the transition of young adult patients with cancer to adult caregiver care is one of the biggest and most important issues [facing pediatric oncology]."

Today, one in every 570 people in the United States who are 20–34 years old is a childhood cancer survivor. Therefore, pediatric oncology care providers need to think about the long-term effects of their treatments on children.

"One of the most important issues for us in pediatric neuro-oncology is how to cure kids without using radiation if at all possible," Britt says. "Many kids with brain tumors have been cured of their primary tumor but at a tremendous cost in terms of their learning and cognitive abilities."

Hooke agrees that a long-term outlook is essential. "Promoting the development of healthy life habits during treatment, such as healthy eating and exercise, is becoming increasingly important and is a great opportunity for nurses," she says.

Helping Terminal Patients

Goodrum adds that end-of-life care also is an important issue being addressed both nationally and within her institution. She feels that "a lack of quality care in the management of the dying child" is a current obstacle to care, a sentiment echoed by Wilson and Nuuhiwa. They identify lack of access to and resources for palliative, home care, and hospice services for pediatric patients with cancer.

Fortunately, as Wilson points out, organizations such as APON are making studies in this area.

"We are seeing increased interest and realization that better education of healthcare professionals is needed regarding pain management and palliative care," she says. To that end, APON is hosting End-of-Life Nurse Education-Pediatric Palliative Care courses and collaborating with the Children's Oncology Group to develop pediatric palliative care guidelines.

Pediatric oncology nurses have developed a deep sense of commitment to their field and a passion for the children and families for whom they care. September is Childhood Cancer Awareness Month; mark your calendars to recognize and support those who do this valuable work.

New Treatments for Breast Cancer

Katherine Hobson

Women face tough choices for the treatment of breast cancer. Surgery to remove the breast (or at least a major portion of it) is one. Chemotherapy is another. For obvious reasons, few women are eager to undergo breast removal, but chemotherapy has had a less-than-stellar record of cures. In the following selection, however, Katherine Hobson describes new treatments that appear to greatly improve the effectiveness of chemotherapy for breast cancer. Use of the drug Herceptin, she reports, has cut the recurrence rate from 33 percent for women treated with standard chemotherapy alone to 15 percent for those using chemotherapy with Herceptin. Other drugs, such as Arimidex and Femara, also promise to reduce the chances that breast cancer will come back after treatment. In cases where recurrence may appear inevitable, another drug, called Avastin, helps to delay the return of cancer by limiting the supply of new blood vessels. The innovations in drug therapies have contributed to a much better situation for breast cancer patients in the first decade of the twenty-first century than those who faced the disease previously.

Katherine Hobson is a senior editor at U.S. News & World Report.

The crowd applauded wildly and wouldn't be quieted. The overflow audience in the Orlando hall was clearly grateful for what it had just heard. One person described it as "mind boggling," another as "jaw dropping," and several said they were on the verge of tears. "It was a Rolling Stones concert in terms of crowd response," says George Sledge, who was on-stage. "Truth to tell, I had a hard time keeping my composure at the end."

But this was no rock concert. Not even close: It was the annual meeting of the American Society of Clinical Oncology, and Sledge, chair of the society's cancer education committee, was leading the discussion at a special session tacked on to the program at the last minute. The topic: a handful of studies looking at a new use of Herceptin, a breast cancer drug previously used to buy time for women whose cancer had spread elsewhere in the body. It was now being studied for use in the early stages of a particularly aggressive form of breast cancer that affects about 50,000 women a year, fully a quarter of women diagnosed with the disease. The Orlando session was the premiere for the kind of hard data that can turn skeptical oncologists into enthusiastic fans.

The researchers onstage got the Mick Jagger treatment for good reason. Herceptin helped a group of women with a specific type of cancer who previously had dim hopes. Science was able to single out these women, but it could offer little help beyond standard treatment. The new research showed that adding the drug to chemotherapy cut the recurrence of cancer by more than half. Put another way, that means that after four years, 15 percent of the women treated with chemo and Herceptin had a recurrence, compared with 33 percent of women treated with chemo alone. "This means major improvements in survival," says Robert Morgan, an oncologist at City of Hope Cancer Center in Duarte, Calif. The drug, he says, will immediately be used in the new way.

New Treatments Proliferating

These women are not out of the woods yet. But the further good news for them is that the Herceptin findings come on the heels of other exciting developments in breast cancer treatment, including new and promising drugs and even news about therapeutic behavior changes, including diet. Add that to a growing understanding of the basic biology of breast cancer and incremental progress in treatment that has been made over the past few years, and the prospects for decreasing the mortality rate further are excellent. "This is a time for huge optimism," says Claudine Isaacs, an oncologist at the Lombardi Comprehensive Cancer Center at Georgetown University.

Yet while there have been huge strides in treating breast cancer—the 10-year survival rate is now about 75 percent and will no doubt climb with the new treatments—challenges remain. A major one is pinpointing women with particular variations of the disease and matching them to the appropriate treatment. As drugs are given to women in earlier stages of their disease, the potential for harmful side effects must be even more carefully considered. And the array of new treatment options means more potential for confusion—and a greater need for women to be more assertive about getting the treatment they need.

Scientists were already on the right track and indeed reported recently in the *Lancet* that middle-aged women treated with chemotherapy and hormonal therapy had their risk of death cut in half over 15 years. The benefit of the chemo and drug therapy increased over time, suggesting that many of them may never have a recurrence. But that news doesn't include the newer variations in chemotherapy introduced over the past several years. Just last week, for example, researchers writing in the *New England Journal of Medicine* reported that replacing an older chemo drug, fluorouracil, with a new one, docetaxel, cut the risk of death by nearly 30 percent among breast cancer patients. Also not yet reflected: even newer drugs, some of which can target specific cancer cells, sparing the rest of the body.

New forms of treatment have now been added to the arsenal, most of them based on a fundamental shift in the way we think about the disease. With recent biological advances, especially in genetics, we now know that—as with other cancers—the term "breast cancer" has actually become somewhat quaint.

More accurate, scientifically, would be "cancers that happen to be in the breast," some of them more aggressive than others.

Changing Scene

A woman diagnosed with breast cancer today [2005] now faces a much different situation from one diagnosed 20, 10, or even five years ago. The debate used to be over which form of chemo to use or how often to use it. Says Sledge: "It was like arguing whether toothpaste A is better than toothpaste B." Doctors now use the "divide and conquer" approach, classifying breast cancers into specific categories and treating them accordingly. Women whose tumors are influenced by the hormones estrogen and progesterone, for example, can benefit from treatments that change the action of those hormones. Many of these women are still treated with tamoxifen—the former gold standard, but not without serious side effects. But a new class of drugs is gaining ground. Aromatase inhibitors [estrogen-reducing drugs], like Arimidex and Femara, were first examined for use after tamoxifen and are now candidates to replace it, at least in some women.

Indeed, one recent study showed that Femara is more effective than tamoxifen in preventing breast cancer recurrence. Those who took the newer drug had a 19 percent lower chance of a recurrence. Since the newer drug has only been in use for six years, it's still too early to know whether it will show a difference in overall survival, says David Epstein, president of the oncology division of Novartis, which makes Femara. One of the patients taking Femara is Joan Syron, a 72-year-old in Annandale, N.J., who was diagnosed with Stage II breast cancer. She started taking Femara in 2001, after five years on tamoxifen, and is still on it. "It's getting to be nine years [after diagnosis], and I'll never really stop worrying," she says, "but I feel comfortable with what I'm doing with my life."

Classified by Protein

Breast cancer tumors can also be classified by whether or not they make too much of a protein called HER2. Women with this type of cancer, who tend to be younger, until quite recently had little help specific to their cancer after completing chemotherapy. "We would see these women and we knew enough to tell them that they had aggressive disease, but we couldn't do anything for them," says Marisa Weiss, an oncologist in Philadelphia and founder of breastcancer.org. Herceptin targets this specific kind of cancer. It was first approved by the Food and Drug Administration for use in the latter stages of breast cancer but later was tested in women with an earlier stage of the disease. When the researchers checked the results after a few years, the successes were so dramatic that they halted the study, arguing it was unethical to deny any patient Herceptin.

That was good news for Marcia Rosenberg, who had been diagnosed with HER2-positive breast cancer after a routine mammogram. It was the first time Rosenberg, a 58-year-old Maryland attorney, had been seriously ill. She recalls hearing the diagnosis: "You could have knocked me over with a feather."

Rosenberg had a lumpectomy and then more surgery before doctors discovered the cancer had spread to her lymph nodes. Isaacs, her oncologist, suggested the Herceptin study, and Rosenberg trusted her. The trial was set up so that all the participants first got four cycles of chemo and then were told which arm of the study they'd been assigned to. Rosenberg learned she'd be assigned to the control group: She wouldn't be getting the drug.

Bad News Reversed

That was devastating news, since the word was out that Herceptin was showing encouraging early results. Isaacs told her to be patient, that some new findings were due out soon.

Rosenberg didn't have to wait more than about 90 minutes: She was in the infusion room, having her chemo treatment, when a nurse handed her the phone and Isaacs told her the good news: The preliminary data looked so good that the patients in the trial, including her, would now be eligible for the drug. "It was one of the most dramatic days of my life," she says.

She's optimistic, and so are oncologists. "Probably thousands of women will be alive in a decade who wouldn't have been otherwise," says Sledge. Still, the study didn't extend long enough to tell if the early benefits will continue. "One must always be cautious looking into the future with these studies," says Len Lichtenfeld, deputy chief medical officer of the American Cancer Society. There are also questions about how long patients should take the drug and in what combinations with other medicines.

And there are still women sitting on the sidelines whose cancers do not fall into the categories treatable with new drugs. "HER2 is the engine that drives this cancer cell, but what are the engines, other than estrogen, that drive these other cells?" asks Karen Gelmon, an oncologist and head of the investigational drug program at the BC Cancer Research Centre in Vancouver.

A Triple Negative Cancer

A new group of women needing even newer treatments is now being talked about: so-called triple negatives, whose cancers aren't estrogen-receptor positive, progesterone-receptor positive, or HER2 positive. Lisa Carey, medical director of the Breast Center at the University of North Carolina, is studying whether this broad group can be subdivided into smaller groups, one of which may respond to drugs like Iressa and Tarceva, which target another receptor known as EGFR. African-American women fall disproportionately into this triple negative category, which may explain why breast cancer in those women tends to occur at younger ages and be more aggressive than in Caucasian women.

The science of classifying tumors this way is still in its rudimentary stage, and even if the statistics show an increase in survival, doctors cannot yet tell an individual patient that she'll survive her cancer for a determined period of time. So the challenge is not only coming up with new treatments but figuring out for whom they do and don't work. One drug that isn't limited to a specific tumor type is Avastin, a drug already shown to help in other cancers by choking off the tumor's blood supply. Genentech and Roche recently reported that in patients with advanced breast cancer, the drug, combined with chemo, doubled the time they lived without a recurrence compared with chemo alone, from six months to 11 months.

Reduction in Tumors

Heraleen Broome's breast cancer had spread to her lungs by 2003, and chemo wasn't working. "I was packing up everything to give it away," the 68-year-old remembers. "And then I decided to unpack and keep my stuff." She joined a trial of Avastin, and 11 tumors in her lungs became three. Every three weeks she drives from her home in Oakland, Calif., to San Francisco for treatment, and the people there are so familiar that it has become a social event.

It's not yet clear whether Avastin will ultimately improve survival rates in breast cancer, but the early reduction in recurrence reminds some of early data on Herceptin. The drug will also be studied in patients with earlier disease. In those early stages, it's not a case of throwing everything at a patient and seeing if it works. For one thing, chemo already has severe side effects. Even the new advance, docetaxel, increases the risk of diarrhea and mouth sores, though it produces less nausea and vomiting. And targeted drugs have their own downsides. Herceptin, for example, can cause heart problems in a small percentage of patients. That's important, since statistically many women who might take the drug would very likely have their cancer driven away by chemotherapy and surgery alone.

Low-Fat Diet May Help

The inevitable risk and expense of drugs explain why doctors were excited about another study, one that suggested for the first time that for some women a low-fat diet might actually reduce the odds that cancer will return. This is the first time that diet has been identified as a tool that survivors can use to protect themselves against the return of cancer; another study showed that even a little exercise can also extend survival (though a healthy lifestyle is no guarantee of beating the disease). "In general, I'm saying to a survivor: There's good data that you should clean up your act after a diagnosis," says Susan Love, a surgeon at the University of California-Los Angeles medical school and author of *Dr. Susan Love's Breast Book*. "Eat a low-fat diet with lots of fruits and vegetables that's low in animal fat." And unlike drugs,there are no potentially hazardous side effects. It's an easy thing for women to do. "To me, it's a no-brainer," says Larry Norton, deputy physician in chief for breast cancer programs at Memorial Sloan-Kettering Cancer Center in New York.

The flood of good news brings complexity to the field of breast cancer and to patients, making early detection and good care crucial. Right from the beginning, it's important to make sure that women have access to screening and proper treatment, says Lichtenfeld. There is also confusion for women struggling to figure out what it all means. Even beyond biology, says Weiss, every woman's breast cancer diagnosis is unique—who she is, how old she is, her social status, her education, her religious beliefs. Her style of making decisions is different, her insurance access is different, and her team of doctors is different.

Staying Informed

With all the developments, "you now need an up-to-date doctor who knows the pros and cons of all these therapies," says John Mendelsohn, president of the M.D. Anderson Cancer Center in Houston. News filters down fast, but Weiss urges newly diagnosed patients to make sure their tumors are tested for hormone receptors and for HER2. Take the time to figure out the best course of treatment for your disease. "There is some sense of urgency, but you don't have to decide overnight what to do," says Weiss. And get a second opinion, suggests Rebecca McMenamin, 43, diagnosed with breast cancer last fall. "Even if you have a great doctor, it's reassuring to hear someone else tell you the same thing."

Whatever the status of the tumor, "patients should seek out opportunities to participate in clinical trials," says Harold Burstein of the Dana-Farber Cancer Institute in Boston. "Getting treated as part of a trial gives you better care—not just because the Herceptin studies were winners but because the care is carefully monitored, it reflects current thinking, and you're getting care that is state of the art." That's true even if you don't end up on the arm of the trial getting the drug— and trial participants will never be given no treatment at all for their cancer. Ask your doctor about trials you might be eligible for, or check out the National Cancer Institute's website for a list. "It's your body—you should learn as much as possible about what is happening and what your options are," advises McMenamin, who joined the Herceptin trial. "That can help to regain a sense of having some control over the situation." (Another benefit: While many women on the trial will now get the drug free, those who weren't may have difficulty being reimbursed for Herceptin, since it hasn't been approved by the FDA [Food and Drug Administration] for its new use.)

Weeks after the scientific meeting that had cancer docs standing and cheering, most have returned home to the day-to-day dramas of treating cancer. But their optimism about progress in the field, though it comes with the caveats necessary in the uncertainty of medicine, lingers.

Attacking Cancer with Vitamin Therapy

Patrick Perry

In the following selection journalist Patrick Perry unveils a novel approach to fighting cancer through vitamin therapy. The approach involves folate, a B vitamin that all cells need. Cancer cells have an extraordinary need for folate, according to researchers, because it is essential for cell division, and the hallmark of a cancer cell is that it divides hundreds or thousands of times faster than a normal cell. The Indiana-based researchers are experimenting with folate combined with a yellow dye called fluorescein, which marks cells for destruction by the body's immune system. According to an interview with one of the investigators involved in the research, the experiments have produced cures in mice. They are hoping to get similar results in human patients.

Patrick Perry is a health journalist who frequently reports on developments in cancer research.

Could the simple vitamin called folate become the most effective warrior in the battle against cancer? . . .

Several years ago, a team of researchers at Purdue University discovered that cancer cells possess a voracious appetite for folate, gobbling up the B vitamin to support rapid cell division—a hallmark of malignant cancer cells. To satisfy this craving, cancer cells developed mechanisms, called folate receptors, to capture folate more effectively than normal cells.

Tricking Cancer Cells to Take Medicine

Researchers are now exploiting cancer cells' craving for the water soluble vitamin by harnessing folate as a therapeutic "Trojan Horse" to sneak cancer-fighting drugs directly into tu-

Patrick Perry, "Outsmarting Cancer with Folate," *Saturday Evening Post*, vol. 274, September 1, 2002, p. 30. Copyright © 2002 Benjamin Franklin Literary and Medical Society. Reproduced by permission.

mor cells. Proceeding unchallenged through the body's immune defense system, folate can attach itself to special folate receptors on the surface of cancer cells, enter the cell with an attached anticancer agent, then wreak havoc on the cancer cell once inside.

"It's using cancer's nutritional needs against itself," says Dr. Philip Low, distinguished professor of chemistry at Purdue, who led the research team that discovered this diagnostic treatment method. "We are essentially slipping medicine in with cancer's favorite food."

The discovery has yielded novel, but complementary anticancer therapies that involve attaching various markers or anticancer agents to folate. One therapy called folate-targeted immunotherapy involves marking or flagging cancer cells and triggering a response from the body's natural immune system.

Alerting the Immune System

"There's no better drug than your own immune system, which consequently is capable of getting rid of every last bacterium, every last virus, or every last fungus in the body. Today's drugs can't do that," says Dr. Christopher Leamon, a member of the Purdue research team and vice president of research at Endocyte, the company developing the new therapies. "Unfortunately, many cancers develop ways to evade immune surveillance. But we've found a way to redirect a patient's immune system to kill those resistant cancer cells by using our folate-target approach."

This method, in effect, forces the body's immune system to fight the disease by marking cancer cells with a foreign agent that triggers an immune response. In chickenpox, for example, the "foreign" virus enters the body, immediately triggering the immune system that summons the body's immune fighting cells to mount an attack. If re-exposed to chickenpox, you won't get the disease because your body has already "seen" it and developed a memory against it; in short, it knows how to fight the disease.

Researchers hope to begin clinical trials using this new approach in late November [2002]. Dr. Low estimates that in the United States alone, about 300,000 people are diagnosed each year with cancers that overexpress the folate receptor, such as ovarian and kidney cancers. In lab studies, the results have been dramatic, with 100 percent cure rates. While initial findings are impressive, researchers are eager to enter into clinical trials late this year.

Interview with a Folate Investigator

To learn more about the unique potential of vitamin-based anticancer therapy, we spoke with Christopher Leamon, Ph.D., at his office in West Lafayette, Indiana.

Q: Could you tell us about the new immunotherapy showing great potential in the battle against cancer in laboratory studies?

A: Endocyte is a small biotech company of about 25 people. Our technology is centered around the use of the vitamin folate for targeting drugs specifically to cancer cells. We achieve that by attaching the drugs chemically to the folic acid itself. Many tumors have evolved a mechanism for grabbing as much folate from the blood as they possibly can in a very efficient way. A protein, called the folate receptor, located on the outer membrane of the cancer cells, is responsible for actually binding the folate.

Normal body tissues do not apparently have this particular protein, or if they do, it is beyond our level of detection. The kidney is one exception. Kidney proximal tubule cells do express the folate receptor on their membranes that face the side of urine collection, but it is believed that the presence of these receptors is not to capture folate for local biological consumption. Rather, these cells merely capture folates prior to their excretion and then transport them back into circulation.

All cells need folate to live, but folate seems to be a very important vitamin for cells to divide. One reason is that the ability of a cell to make DNA is dependent upon the vitamin folate. You can imagine a cancer cell that divides every 18 to 24 hours needs to double its amount of DNA in a very short time. To do that, it needs folate. Without folate, it will not divide that quickly. Certain cancers, not all—and that is an important point to make—will express this high affinity folate receptor as a means by which they can preferentially take in as much folate from the bloodstream as needed to support tumor growth. It is an aggressive, stingy way of doing that, but that is what the cancer cells do. Normal cells also require folate to maintain normal biochemistry, but they have another way of getting the folate inside which is very different from what we are doing. This other mechanism is a much weaker, less efficient way of getting folate, but again normal cells do not need as much folate for survival because they are not dividing at the rate cancer cells do, if at all.

Folate Triggers the Immune System

Because cancer has this protein which can bind folate very effectively, it is very specific interaction—sort of like a key going into a lock. We attach compounds to folate, and whatever we attach will also bind to the cancer cell by virtue of folate's ability to bind to the folate receptors. Again, picture folate as the key, and there is a little loop in the key. On that loop, you can attach, for example, a key ring. Picture that key ring as the drug. The drug itself has nothing to do with turning that lock, because the key—folate—is turning the lock. In other words, folate is binding to the cancer cell by virtue of that receptor, or protein, but the drug is coming along for the ride because it is attached to folate.

We have found throughout the course of many years of research that we can deliver molecules that are attached to folate inside the cell. The cell will absorb drugs attached to folate. We can also get very good biochemical responses. If we design to kill a cell, we can kill it with the right drug. However, we also found that a significant fraction of what is associated with the cancer cell—the folate/drug combination—actually remains on the cell surface at any given time. The reason for that, it is believed, is that the cell will internalize, or absorb, the amount of folate that it needs to satisfy its biochemical activity. And what the cell doesn't need immediately is then stored on the cell surface.

This is the key to our immunotherapy. By having folate on the cell surface, we believed we could exploit this in some way to flag the tumor cell. In other words, we wanted a project in the field of immunology where we would deliver a certain molecular flag to the tumor cell that would then get the immune system interested in fighting the tumor. In these experiments, instead of attaching a drug to folate, we simply attached a harmless, yellow dye called fluorescein. This yellow dye, or fluorescein, binds to folate on the tumor cell. You are left with the cell basically decorated with this fluorescein molecule on the cell surface.

If the patient has immunity against the fluorescein, his or her immune system will generate antibodies against it. And those antibodies, present in the body's bloodstream, will recognize the tumor cell coated with the yellow dye. The antibody then recruits the immune system's infection-fighting cells to come in and kill the tumor cell. The reason the process works is because we are artificially giving the tumor cell an antigen that the immune system can recognize and mount an attack against. It is basically a molecular flag, telling the immune system, "Here we are. Come fight us." It works very effectively in our mouse models.

Vaccine-Plus-Therapy Approach

Q: Is this a whole new approach to cancer therapy?

A: It is a very different approach. It is actually a fusion approach because we are combining a vaccine with a drug therapy. We are cautioning everyone that we did generate cures, but the reality is, these cures were in mice, and what we see in mice may not translate as effectively into the clinic with humans. We are very optimistic, but we have to determine the potential in the clinic.

The unique thing that we found with this combination vaccine-plus-therapy approach was that not only were the laboratory mice cured of the cancer, but a "memory" had developed. For example, once we established that the mice were cured, we reinjected them with the original tumor cells that normally would kill the animal after 21 days. But when these "cured" animals received a subsequent injection of tumor cells—what we call rechallenge—they had survived. More importantly, they survived without any further treatment. We believe what happened was that memory developed, just like when you were a child and exposed to chickenpox. After exposure, if a child with chickenpox came and coughed in your face, you would not get chickenpox because your body had already seen it and developed memory against it; it knows how to fight that disease. Our approach is similar. Once we train the immune system to fight that tumor, it will develop a memory so that if that tumor came up again, the memory cells would go and fight it directly.

Q: Is the yellow dye, fluorescein, used in other procedures?

A: Fluorescein is a fluorescent molecule used very commonly in biochemistry to label molecules, like proteins. You can actually look under a fluorescence microscope and see where that molecule is within a cell. It's a visual tracer.

You can use it for a number of applications. It is a very common compound in the lab, and we knew that if presented to the immune system as a vaccine formulation, immunity against fluorescein would develop. We initially decided to try it for our model studies. Originally when we began this project, we were going to try to use short pieces of common pathogens, like tetanus toxin, because everyone is immunized against tetanus. However, we quickly realized that fluorescein produced the necessary immunological activity that we needed, so we simply decided to develop our vaccine with it.

Prostate Cancer and Its Treatments

Carol Rados

The prostate is found only in men, where it produces the milky medium that contains semen. In the following selection health journalist Carol Rados explains how the prostate can become a troublesome, even deadly, threat to a man's health later in life. As men age, she explains, three kinds of problems can afflict the prostate. The first two, infection and enlargement, can be cured or managed. The third, however, is cancer of the prostate. As cancers go, it is slow moving, but since it is hard to detect (current tests are only partially reliable), it poses a threat of spreading to other parts of the body, at which point risk of dying becomes greatly elevated. Treatment can include removal of the prostate by surgery. However, this may leave the patient impotent. Other treatments include radiation and chemotherapy. Meantime, research continues into better methods of detection.

Carol Rados is a staff writer for FDA Consumer *magazine.*

To screen, or not to screen: that is the question. Whether men should get tested for prostate cancer when they have no symptoms is a long-running debate within the medical community.

There is good evidence, according to the Centers for Disease Control and Prevention (CDC), that the current prostate specific antigen (PSA) test approved in 1986 by the Food and Drug Administration [FDA] to screen for prostate cancer can detect the disease in its early stages. Evidence, however, is mixed and inconclusive about whether early detection actually saves lives. A study published in the Jan. 9, 2006, issue of the *Archives of Internal Medicine* found that screening with the

Carol Rados, "Prostate Health: What Every Man Needs to Know," *FDA Consumer*, May 1, 2006. p. 18. Reproduced by permission.

PSA test does not cut down on deaths from the disease. Moreover, it is not clear whether the benefits of screening outweigh the risks of follow-up testing and cancer treatments.

At the same time, evidence, such as a drop in the prostate cancer death rate—which some say could be due to improved treatments—suggests that early PSA testing may be saving lives. There are no definitive answers.

According to the National Cancer Institute (NCI), other than skin cancer, prostate cancer is the most common form of cancer and the second leading cause of cancer-related deaths among men in the United States. But doctors' recommendations on screening for the disease vary. Some encourage annual screenings for men older than age 50; others recommend against routine screening. American Cancer Society (ACS) Screening Director Robert Smith, Ph.D., says that the January *Archives of Internal Medicine* study "isn't strong enough to say definitively that prostate cancer screening isn't valuable."

The controversy, meanwhile, is contributing to a growing quandary for doctors and their patients: what's a man to do?

Until there is more evidence and, perhaps, a scientific consensus of the screening benefits, most doctors and medical organizations, including the NCI, the ACS, and the CDC, agree that men should learn all they can about what is known and what is not known of the benefits and limitations of early detection and treatment for prostate cancer, so that they can make their own informed decisions.

The Pesky Prostate

Cancer screening is just one health concern related to the prostate—a very important part of the male reproductive system. As men age, the prostate may become a source of troubling, often inconvenient problems that can, but don't necessarily, include cancer. And since the symptoms of some noncancerous prostate conditions can mimic cancer, many men who learn they have a problem often assume the worst.

In general, growing older raises a man's risk for prostate problems, including cancer. . . .

For these reasons, it is important that men know and understand, in the earliest stages, the changes that can occur in the prostate and could, ultimately, affect their health.

The prostate is a walnut-shaped gland found only in men. It lies in front of the rectum, sits just below the bladder where urine is stored, and surrounds the tube that carries urine from the body (urethra). The gland functions as part of the male reproductive system by making a fluid that becomes part of semen, the white fluid that contains sperm.

Variety of Problems

Three main problems can occur in the prostate gland: inflammation or infection, called prostatitis; enlargement, called benign prostatic hyperplasia (BPH); and cancer.

Prostatitis is a clinical term used to describe a wide spectrum of disorders from acute bacterial infection to chronic pain syndromes affecting the prostate, says Regina Alivisatos, M.D., a medical officer in the FDA's Center for Drug Evaluation and Research (CDER). . . .

BPH, or benign prostatic hyperplasia, is the second main problem that can occur in the prostate. "Benign" means "not cancerous"; "hyperplasia" means "too much growth." The result is that the prostate becomes enlarged. The gland tends to expand in an area that doesn't expand with it, causing pressure on the urethra, which can lead to urinary problems.

The urge to urinate frequently, a weak urine flow, breaks in urine stream, and dribbling are all symptoms of an enlarged prostate. Because the prostate normally continues to grow as a boy matures to manhood, BPH is the most common prostate problem for men older than 50. Older men are at risk for prostate cancer as well, but it is much less common than BPH. . . .

Different prostate problems sometimes have similar symptoms, according to the National Institute of Diabetes and Digestive and Kidney Diseases (NIDDK). For example, one man with prostatitis and another with BPH may both have a frequent, urgent need to urinate. A man with BPH may have trouble beginning a stream of urine; another may have to urinate frequently at night. Or, a man in the early stages of prostate cancer may have no symptoms at all.

But according to the NCI, one prostate change does not lead to another. For example, having prostatitis or an enlarged prostate does not increase the chance for prostate cancer. It is also possible to have more than one condition at a time. This confusing array of potential scenarios makes a case for the importance of all men, especially after age 45, to have a thorough medical exam that includes the PSA test and DRE [digital rectal exam] every year. . . .

A Hidden Threat

The third major problem that can occur in the prostate is cancer. It grows quietly for years, giving most men with the early disease no obvious symptoms.

"It's a silent killer," says J. Brantley Thrasher, M.D., chairman of urology at the University of Kansas Medical Center in Kansas City, Kan., and spokesman for the American Urological Association (AUA). "So, most men with a nodule or elevated PSA aren't going to know it." That's why Thrasher and the AUA believe strongly in PSA testing. "It's an imperfect marker, but it's the best we've got."

The FDA approved the PSA test for use in conjunction with a DRE to help detect prostate cancer in men 50 and older, and for monitoring prostate cancer patients after treatment. According to scientists in the FDA's Center for Devices and Radiological Health (CDRH), the finger examination can detect cancer in the form of a nodule or hardness, normally when it is about 50 percent advanced and not curable. PSA detects cancer when the finger exam appears normal in about 35 percent to 40 percent of cases, in the early stages of disease.

Indeed, the NCI and the ACS agree that checking people for some cancers, such as breast and colon, even when they have no symptoms, can reduce deaths by finding tumors at an early stage, when they are easiest to treat. But when it comes to prostate cancer, the argument isn't so clear-cut.

"Prostate cancer is generally a slow-growing cancer," says Cmdr. James P. Reeves, Ph.D., a medical device reviewer in the FDA's CDRH. "For those men who do not have slow-growing cancer that will threaten their lives, we do not have sufficient information that PSA or DRE testing prior to or after diagnosis would distinguish such men from those who will have cancer, but will not die from that cancer."

Testing Can Bring Trouble

So what's the harm in being tested? Reeves says that screening for prostate cancer sometimes finds tumors that wouldn't cause any problems if left untreated. Many professional medical organizations agree. But there's no good way at this time to tell which cancers need treating and which don't. Therefore, many men who are diagnosed with prostate cancer likely will be treated, but also may experience unnecessary and harmful side effects that could lower their quality of life. About 15 percent to 50 percent of men treated for prostate cancer by surgery, radiation therapy, or hormonal therapy will have urinary incontinence and sexual impotence, and in extremely rare cases, scarring of the intestine.

"These percentages indicate that there is a risk for significant harm from over-treatment of prostate cancer," Reeves says. "Is the cure worse than the disease, especially if the cancer is not significant enough to threaten a man's life over 10 to 15 years of remaining life expectancy?"

There are some men who have ample reason to choose the cure. "My grandfather and my father had prostate cancer," says 54-year-old David Glunt from St. Louis. "And at 51 years old, I wasn't taking any chances." Glunt's younger brother tested positive for prostate cancer four years ago; Glunt tested negative. "But I was betting all along that I would get it," he says. A year later, he did.

Speaking on behalf of the AUA, Thrasher says that while a more specific and sensitive marker is needed, questioning the validity of early screening puts men at risk. "Physicians should discuss the risks and benefits of prostate cancer screening on a yearly basis with men 50 to 75 years of age, and earlier if they are African-American or have a family history of prostate cancer," Thrasher says. Screening, he adds, should include both a PSA test and DRE.

Because so much remains unknown about how to interpret the PSA test, its ability to discriminate between cancer and noncancerous conditions, and the best course of action if the PSA is high, the magnitude of the test's potential risks and benefits also is unknown.

Still, Kibel adds, "the PSA controversy should not stop men from discussing being tested with their doctors."

Treatment Saves Lives

In its early stages, prostate cancer stays in the prostate and is not life-threatening. But without treatment, cancer eventually spreads to other parts of the body, often resulting in death.

Doctors have several ways to treat prostate cancer. The choice depends on many factors, such as whether or not the cancer has spread beyond the prostate, the patient's age and general health, and how the patient feels about the treatment options and their side effects. According to both the NCI and the ACS, approaches to treatment include: watchful waiting to see whether the cancer is growing slowly and not causing symptoms; surgery to remove the entire prostate and surrounding tissues; and internal and external radiation therapy, both of which use high-energy rays to kill cancer cells and shrink tumors. Hormone therapy and chemotherapy drugs are approved to treat the various advanced stages of cancer.

The gold standard for treating early, localized prostate cancer is radical retropubic prostatectomy. The whole prostate and seminal vesicles are removed. At Johns Hopkins Hospital in Baltimore, the surgery has improved over the years with the development of a nerve-sparing procedure. This procedure, says the CDRH, in most cases, avoids sexual impotence. The same technique has been used in the last decade by many urologists in the United States and throughout the world.

Computer- or robot-assisted surgery was cleared by the FDA in 2005 for use in all urological procedures, including the removal of the prostate (radical prostatectomy) because of cancer. Even though the prostate is surrounded by nerves and muscles that affect urinary, rectal, and sexual functions, doctors say that improved vision and flexibility of the instruments allow for magnification of the prostate during this procedure. "It's too early to tell if this will equate to more precision and better outcomes," adds Thrasher.

Regular checkups are important even for men who have had surgery. . . .

Research is under way to evaluate new approaches to finding even more effective treatments for prostate and urinary disorders.

How PSA Signals Cancer

Prostate specific antigen (PSA) is a substance made by the prostate gland. Although the substance is mostly found in semen, a small amount is also present in the blood. According to the American Cancer Society, most men have levels under 4 nanograms per milliliter of blood (ng/ml). When prostate cancer develops, the PSA level usually goes above 4ng/ml but in some cases, the cancer can be present at levels lower than 4.

A PSA rise does not automatically mean cancer. PSA also rises when the prostate is enlarged because of benign prostatic hyperplasia, or BPH, and sometimes with prostatitis.

If the level is borderline range between 4ng/ml and 10ng/ml, a man has about a 25 percent to 35 percent chance of having prostate cancer. PSA higher than 10ng/ml could mean between a 40 percent and 50 percent chance for cancer, and the risk increases further as the PSA level increases. PSA is an ideal marker for prostate cancer because it is basically restricted to prostate cells.

Most PSA tests measure "total PSA," or the amount that is bound to blood proteins. But some tests measure not only total PSA, but another component called free PSA, which floats unbound in the blood. Free PSA above 25 percent is a stronger indication that cancer is not present. Comparing the two helps doctors rule out cancer in men whose PSA is mildly elevated from other causes.

The benefits of screening for prostate cancer are still being studied. Scientists are researching ways to distinguish between cancerous and noncancerous conditions, those that are slow-growing and fast-growing, and potentially lethal cancers through new PSA methods and other tumor markers.

The National Cancer Institute and other medical organizations are conducting the Prostate, Lung, Colorectal, and Ovarian Cancer Screening Trial, or PLCO Trial, to determine whether certain screening tests reduce the number of deaths from these cancers. The PSA and DRE tests are being studied to see whether yearly screening will decrease a man's chance of dying from prostate cancer.

Unconventional Cancer Treatments

Georgia Decker

Cancer is a difficult disease to treat. Often, conventional thera-pies fall short of a full cure or fail altogether. Many cancer pa-tients consider complementary or alternative therapies. In the following selection oncology nurse Georgia Decker explains the difference between complementary and alternative medicine (CAM) therapies and the roles they play in the treatment of cancer. The first, she explains, accompanies conventional science-based medicine, while the latter substitutes for it. CAM embraces a wide variety of treatments, ranging from meditation to special diets, and from herbal supplements to acupuncture. The key point about CAM therapies is that they have not been subjected to the rigorous proving methods that conventional medicines are required to undergo. However, this does not mean they are use-less. Rather, it means that scientific testing may or may not pro-vide evidence of safety and utility in the future.

Georgia Decker is a nurse with more than two decades of ex-perience in cancer wards, where both conventional and CAM therapies have been employed.

Complementary and alternative medicine (CAM), also known as *integrative medicine*, is the language currently used by the National Institutes of Health (NIH). Medical jour-nals now include information about CAM therapies being re-searched.

Some authors say that a common reason for using these therapies is a patient's disappointment with conventional therapies. Others state that it is a perception of improved quality of life and an increased sense of control that appeals to patients. Patients want to be treated in a holistic way with what they consider to be natural or nontoxic remedies. These therapies may be used when conventional therapies fail, during conventional therapy, or when a patient seeks more control in his or her health care. From 1990 to 1997, the use of CAM therapies increased 25 percent, the use of herbal medicine increased 380 percent, and the use of high-dose vitamins increased 130 percent. Unfortunately, less than 40 percent of CAM therapies used were disclosed to a physician in 1990 and 1997. This low rate of disclosure is of concern to health care professionals. A survey conducted in 2000 of CAM therapy use by cancer patients participating in clinical trials revealed that most used at least one type of CAM therapy: spirituality (94 percent); imagery (86 percent); massage (80 percent); lifestyle, diet, nutrition (60 percent); relaxation (50 percent); herbal/botanical (20 percent); and high-dose vitamins (14 percent).

Differing Meanings

The use of *complementary* and *alternative* as meaning the same thing has led to miscommunication and confusion. These terms are not interchangeable. They describe the intent with which a therapy is used, not the therapy itself.

A therapy is *alternative* when it is used in place of conventional therapy. An example is a patient using only herbs as a treatment for cancer. *Complementary therapies* are those used in addition to or to complement conventional therapy, such as the use of meditation in addition to combat nausea. The more contemporary term *integrative* means combining conventional and unconventional therapies in a way that is safe and supervised, and with a result that is better than a result of either one used alone. What one person may consider conventional may not be conventional to another person. Culture, ethnicity, and previous experience affect what you consider conventional. It is very important that you communicate with your health care providers regarding any therapies that you are using.

Although the use of CAM therapies has grown in the United States and internationally, little is known about the safety and efficacy of many therapies, especially when used by a person receiving cancer therapy. The National Institutes of Health National Center for Complementary and Alternative Medicines (NIH-NCCAM) was created in 1998 to "facilitate the evaluation of alternative medical treatment modalities" to determine their effectiveness. The NHI-NCCAM does not provide referrals for CAM therapies or practitioners. It does conduct and support research and training, and provides information on CAM therapies to practitioners and the public. . . .

CAM Techniques and Treatments

Important caution: The symptoms of mental illness may worsen with some of these modalities. Therefore, choosing a therapist who is skilled in these therapies, as well as knowledgeable about physical and mental illnesses, is very important.

Relaxation and *meditation* are techniques that include a variety of modalities, including breath therapy, hypnotherapy, imagery and visualization, meditation, and yoga. Some authors include Tai Chi in this category. Although they vary in methodology, all require a quiet, stress-free environment. Patients have reported positive outcomes, including increased happiness and self-confidence.

Imagery and *visualization* may be referred to as guided imagery, creative imagery, or visualization therapy. These techniques incorporate the use of images or symbols and focus the mind on bodily functions. Imagery and visualization have been used successfully to decrease stress, pain, and heart rate. Recent studies have shown that these therapies may stimulate the immune system. Although imagery is used as a self-help technique, initial practice should be under the guidance of a therapist who is skilled in this technique, as well as knowledgeable about medical and psychiatric conditions.

Music therapy is the intentional use of music or sound— writing music or listening to music to impact health. Practitioners of sound therapy, a subset of music therapy, believe the use of sound waves can restore body harmony. They may work with individuals or groups. Music therapy has been used in mental health care, stress management, and pain management. Choose a qualified music therapist to lessen the chance of having an unexpected problem.

Bioelectromagnetic Therapies

Acupuncture is an expression of electromagnetic pathways of body energy flow. The Meridian System, the primary map of the body used by acupuncturists, describes energy channels flowing throughout the body. Acupuncturists use 12 principal meridians and 365 points *(acupoints)*. When acupuncture needles are placed at an acupoint, you may feel a slight ache, dull pain, or tingling sensation that lasts a few seconds. Once the needle is in place, you should feel no discomfort. In fact, some patients report a sensation of warmth. An acupoint may be stimulated in a number of ways. For example, crystals can be used instead of needles. Acupuncture is most widely used for a specific purpose, such as pain management or immune-system balancing. However, patients are treated as a whole with an understanding that signs and symptoms are interrelated. Acupuncture has been scientifically proven to decrease pain and is included in pain management guidelines.

Magnet therapy is based on the theory that the body consists of various energy processes that generate their own magnetic field and that the manipulation of these fields has therapeutic potential. Magnet energy as a cause of and potential cure for disease has been a topic of fascination for health care professionals for many years. Two types of magnets can be used. Electromagnets conduct electrical currents through wire. Permanent magnets create a magnetic field when the electrons in the atoms of the magnet are in motion. Magnets are said to have been used successfully in the treatment of peripheral neuropathies [damage to nerves outside the brain and spinal cord] and pain syndromes. Research in this therapy is increasing.

Herbal Medicine

The United States Food and Drug Administration (FDA) lists approximately 250 herbs as GRAS (generally recognized as safe). Only six herbs (aloe, capsicum, cascara psyllium, senna, and witch hazel) received FDA approval before the passage of the Dietary Supplement Health and Education Act of 1994. Under this law, herbs in the United States are now classified and sold as nutritional supplements and no longer require FDA approval. The active ingredient content of these products is not controlled or standardized. A constant concern is the purity of the product. A 1998 study conducted by the California Department of Health found that some herbal products are contaminated with heavy metals as well as other substances. In 1997, an estimated 15 million adults took prescription medications concurrently with herbal remedies and/or high-dose vitamins. These individuals are at risk for potential adverse drug-herb or drug-supplement interactions.

Medicinal herbs can interact with pharmaceuticals. Herbs should be discontinued if any unpleasant side effects occur. *When in doubt, do without.* Most herbs have specific indications and therefore should not be taken in particular situations.

More information about potential interactions between herbs and drugs is available from the Food and Drug Administration at www.fda.org (click on "Medwatch").

Pharmacological and Biological Therapies

Oxidative therapies are based upon the belief that cancer and viruses cannot exist in an oxygen-rich environment. Oxygen is essential to life; some people believe that oxygen deficiency is a component of illness. Oxidative therapies are believed to improve oxygen concentration and thus fight illness, including cancer. Hydrogen peroxide infusions and ozone are examples of oxidative therapies. Although research is being conducted regarding these therapies, they remain controversial.

Colostrum has been used to treat diarrhea, to improve gastrointestinal health, and to boost the immune system. Colostrum, the first milk new mothers secrete after giving birth, is a rich natural source of nutrients, antibodies, and growth factors for a newborn. Several studies show that bovine colostrum concentrates are highly successful in improving gastrointestinal health and in treating certain kinds of diarrhea. Product purity is a major concern. Potential side effects include mild gastrointestinal upset, mild nausea, and flatulence.

Laetrile (also known as amygdalin, Vitamin B17)— Amygdalin is a cyanide-containing substance that was once believed to be, *but has since been disproven as*, an effective cancer therapy. Laetrile is a concentrated form of amygdalin. It is usually administered intravenously, but also has been injected into an artery immediately above the tumor site. It may also be taken orally. There are documented reports of accidental poisoning with laetrile tablets. Potential side effects include weakness, dizziness, nausea, vomiting, diarrhea, and fever.

Shark cartilage and bovine cartilage are believed to inhibit the formation of blood vessels to and within the tumor, and to enhance the immune system. Studies are currently testing the effectiveness of shark cartilage in these two areas. The original theory was based on the observation that sharks do not appear to get cancer. Sharks do get cancer, however. Shark or bovine cartilage is used as an oral preparation. It is expensive and product purity is a concern. Potential side effects include mild gastrointestinal upset and flatulence.

Manual Healing Methods

Massage therapy is the specific manipulation of the body's soft tissues. Massage therapists use their hands, but sometimes forearms, elbows, and feet as well. The touch used in massage involves varying degrees of pressure. Massage therapy can be used in a variety of ways, but it has been controversial for cancer survivors. Fear of spreading cancer has kept many cancer patients and survivors from receiving massage. Only certain types of massage are appropriate in certain situations. For example, massage directly over a tumor or surgical site is not appropriate. It is important to seek a massage therapist who is knowledgeable about cancer and its therapies. The key effects of massage include: 1) improved digestion, 2) increased range of motion, 3) improved lymphatic movement and circulation, 4) decreased muscle tension, and 5) decreased edema.

"*Reiki*" means universal life energy. It is an ancient healing art derived from the Japanese in which the healer is thought to manipulate energy. The energy, not the practitioner, effects healing. The practitioner will hold his or her hands in a series of positions on the patient but no pressure or massage is applied. The patient remains fully clothed at all times. The energy is believed to find its way wherever and however it is needed. The purpose of Reiki is to relieve the body of physical, emotional, and spiritual blockages. Healing also takes place on the emotional, mental, and spiritual levels, rather than only on the physical level. The environment is kept as quiet and soothing as possible. Reiki has been used for pain, nausea and other gastrointestinal disturbances, and in stress management.

Reflexology is the practice of applying specific pressure to specific points on the feet and/or hands. The pressure may vary from heavy to light depending on the practitioner. It is holistic because it looks at the needs of the whole body. Reflexology is more than a foot massage. The exact mechanism as to how reflexology works is not clear, but it is believed to restore balance to the body by restoring the flow of energy. Reflexology can be used for gastrointestinal problems, stress-related problems, chronic pain, and fatigue. . . .

Dietary Therapy

The *Gonzalez-Kelley* (or *Kelley-Gonzalez*) regimen is being studied at one of the NIH-designated research centers. It is based on the work of Donald Kelley, who believed that alterations in the body's proteins can result in cancer. Nicolas Gonzalez has evaluated Kelley's work and found that by applying Kelley's theory, many of his patients with pancreatic cancer had improved survival rates.

This regimen is composed of 10 basic diets. As with other nutritional programs, this regimen should be medically supervised to avoid complications such as protein malnutrition and other nutritional deficiencies.

Nutritional supplements have become popular because of the appeal of "natural" in treating or preventing disease. Megavitamin therapies appeal to many patients, although they have not yet proved to be effective. Much has been written about diet and its effect on health and disease. Recently more Americans are taking nutritional supplements. Many medical experts are reluctant to recommend nutritional supplements, and the recommended dosages will vary from practitioner to practitioner. . . .

A Personal Choice

Choosing to use a CAM therapy is a very personal decision. It must feel right to you. Research does not prove which therapies are right. Many well-meaning friends and acquaintances will offer advice about a therapy based on personal experience or the experience of a friend or relative. Each is physically and emotionally unique; you cannot assume that if a particular therapy was the right one for your neighbor, it will be the right one for you, too. For example, one person can take a certain antibiotic and another person cannot. Not all CAM therapies will complement your cancer therapies. . . .

You cannot ensure that your CAM practitioner and oncologist will work together. Survivors and health care providers are learning more about these therapies every day, but still have much to learn. In many cases, cancer survivors, oncologists, oncology nurses, and other members of the health care team are learning at the same time. Ask your CAM practitioners for written information about their particular therapy and a copy of any treatment plan they made for you. Give both to your oncologist to put in your medical record. Should any members of your health care team need additional information, they can, with your permission, contact the CAM practitioner. This creates an opportunity for communication, which can lead to collaboration.

Do not keep your CAM therapy a secret from your oncologist. A particular therapy may not be known to be safe during cancer treatment, but may pose no risk after the cancer treatment has been completed. Similarly, a particular therapy may be considered safe during treatment for one cancer diagnosis, but not known to be safe or unsafe for another diagnosis. *Safety trumps efficacy* is the advice offered by Dr. David Eisenberg of Harvard. That is, a particular therapy may be effective for a particular symptom, but it may not be safe for this particular person, at this particular time, under these particular circumstances.

CONTEMPORARY
ISSUES
COMPANION

CHAPTER 3

Personal Experiences with Cancer

Losing a Womb, Gaining a Cause

Tamika Felder

In the following selection African American television producer Tamika Felder describes her encounters with cancer. They began when she was growing up in an affectionate family within a tight-knit community in Summerville, South Carolina. As Tamika approached her seventeenth birthday, her father fell gravely ill with colon cancer. The day before Tamika's birthday, her beloved father died. Eight years later, Tamika was diagnosed with cervical cancer. The disease was so advanced that she had to undergo a total hysterectomy. Tamika survived the treatment but can never bear children. She urges all women to get an HPV (human papillomavirus) test and a Pap smear once a year.

My mother is the sort who calls me just to ask, "What did you eat today, and while you're watching TV, can't you do some leg lifts?" Mom's vigilance is born of loss: Name a type of cancer, and she can name the relative who has suffered with it. In 1992 my father succumbed to colon cancer. "Daddy, please don't die on my birthday," I begged when the doctors gave him only days to live. "Baby girl." he whispered, "I won't." A week later, my father passed away, having kept his promise. The next morning, I began my seventeenth year of life without him.

By the time I was 24, I had landed a job as an associate producer for a political cable network. I covered the presidential campaign, hobnobbed with celebrities, and interviewed leaders such as Hillary Clinton and Al Gore. My apartment became a pit stop between plane rides and 14-hour workdays.

My life couldn't have been more exhilarating—until the morning in 2001 when I woke up with an excruciating pain under my right armpit. In that armpit, a zit the size of a pea had grown to a red knot the size of a golf ball. The doctor in the ER recognized the lump as a pus-filled boil caused by antiperspirant that had clogged my pores. He cut open the abscess, drained it, stuffed it with gauze, and then sent me home sore. A few days later, he referred me to a surgeon who could remove what was left of the boil. I'm here today because of that referral.

After performing a laser operation, the surgeon asked. "When was your last physical?" I admitted I hadn't seen a doctor for two years. Then I revealed a secret humiliation: The last time I'd gone for a Pap smear, the doctor made a comment I couldn't forget. "Your stomach is so big, you wouldn't even know if you were pregnant," she exclaimed. At the time, I was about 50 pounds overweight, and her words, along with the thought of the cold speculum and stirrups, had been enough to keep me away from getting a pelvic exam ever since.

"My wife is a family practitioner," the surgeon said kindly. "Why don't you go see her?" Soon after, I met his spouse, a fiftyish Armenian with a voice that could simultaneously admonish and reassure. Instantly we connected. After I gave her my family health history, she tested me from scalp to toenail. She then performed a Pap smear and scheduled a follow-up visit.

I stopped in for my results before work two days later. "You don't have diabetes," my physician told me. Exhale. "No high blood pressure or cholesterol, either." I stood, smoothed out the jacket of my gray suit, and reached for my purse. But the doctor nudged me back into the chair. "Now," she said, her voice softening at the edges, "let's talk about this Pap test." I froze. My spirit seemed to lift out of my body and waft up toward the ceiling. "Tamika, you have cervical cancer."

Before the doctor could utter another syllable, I grabbed my purse and keys and raced toward the door. "Come here, sweetie," she persuaded as she followed me through the lobby. Outside, the cool air hit my face as hot tears tumbled. "It's okay," the doctor said again and again while I sobbed. "You'll be fine."

We returned to the office, where she sedated me and contacted a specialist she hoped could perform a biopsy immediately. My mother, who just happened to be visiting from South Carolina, came with me to the specialist. Lying on the table after the doctor snipped off a piece of my cervix, I overheard him tell the nurse how badly I was bleeding. I lifted my head and peered at his face. He offered a grin that felt like a tie.

A few days later, my doctor confirmed that I indeed had advanced malignant carcinoma in my cervix. "How did this happen?" I asked through tears. "You probably had genital warts [caused by HPV] first," she said. At that moment, I stopped crying, because any of my friends can tell you that I'm up on my STDs. I preach safe sex and even jokingly warn my pals to use plastic wrap on the parts of the penis the latex doesn't cover. So I can assure you that if I had a cauliflower-like wart growing on my genitals, I would've noticed. I had never once had intercourse without using a condom, nor had I risked my health through promiscuity. I left my doctor's office that day carrying a brew of guilt (why hadn't I continued having my annual Paps?), shame (just hearing the word *wart* made me feel like a leper) and unanswered questions.

I would soon learn that HPV stands for human papillomavirus—a sexually transmitted infection that affects nearly 20 million Americans. Condom use might serve as a barrier, but because this STI is transmitted by skin-to-skin contact, "safe sex" can't guarantee protection. Only abstinence can do that. Though HPV doesn't necessarily lead to cervical cancer, nearly all women diagnosed with carcinoma of the cervix have HPV. Some strains cause vaginal warts, other strains cause cancer, but thousands of carriers never see a single symptom. The only way to know for certain whether you have HPV is to ask your gynecologist for an HPV test in addition to a yearly Pap smear. *You must insist on that HPV test.* Though early detection won't eradicate the virus, discovering you have it will give you the chance to control and alleviate symptoms.

Over the next two weeks, Mom tried to comfort me. "Are you warm enough?" she'd ask in a voice that said, "I love you." But she eventually had to return home to South Carolina. The day I visited Johns Hopkins Hospital for another test and learned that I would need a hysterectomy, she had already left, and I was alone. "If we don't remove the cancer soon," the doctor told me, "you could lose your life." I panicked. As career-driven as I am, I've always wanted children. Like so many professional women, I had a life map that looked something like this: work in my 20s and early 30s, marry by 35, squeeze in some world travel, have kids sometime around 40. A hysterectomy wasn't part of that plan. So I sought a second opinion, and then a third. I finally accepted the truth from a Black doctor at Howard University Hospital in Washington, D.C. "Get the surgery right away," she told me. I was 25.

On June 14, 2001, with my mom at my side, I returned to Johns Hopkins for a full hysterectomy. I went home after the operation with staples down my abdomen. In excruciating pain, I developed a terrible fever. An MRI revealed a blood clot. The doctor had to remove ten of my staples so he could drain the clot. You have never heard a woman scream like I did! In the following weeks, as the incision healed, I felt empty and incomplete. I could literally sense the loss of my uterus. It was as if my ovaries were jiggling around inside me, attached to nothing. I felt as if an important part of me had died.

Even now, whenever I touch a pregnant woman's stomach, I always think, *I'll never know what it's like to carry a child.* As happy as I might be for the expectant mother, I still mourn my own loss. Therapy became my refuge, a chance to take off the mask and speak honestly about my experience. My greatest fear is that I'll never find a husband, a man who can accept a woman who is barren. But then I tell myself, *You're special, Tamika. For whatever reason, this is your journey. Embrace it.*

For a while I tried to resume life as I'd once known it—chasing hot assignments, plotting my ascent in the television business, traveling nonstop. But I couldn't get HPV off my mind. If my virus had been caught sooner, even a year or two before, it's possible my uterus might have been saved. I wanted to tell other women that cervical cancer can be prevented. Even though about 3,700 women die each year from cervical carcinoma, you don't have to lose your womb or your life to the disease. You just have to keep what I call the Eleventh Commandment: No matter how busy or broke you think you are, whether you have insurance or not, you must never, *ever* skip your yearly Pap smear and HPV test.

Every year I celebrate what I call my Rebirthday. I lost my uterus June 14 but gained a second chance at living. I believe I was spared so I could honor my father's memory and leave you with this: Get tested annually. It could save your life.

(Tamika Felder created TamikaAndFriends.org, a cyber gathering spot where women can share stories about their sexual lives and cancer survivors can connect with one another.)

A Parent's Perspective

Steve Pettey

In the following selection a dad records his impressions as his ten-year-old son Gordon is diagnosed and treated for a brain tumor. Steve Pettey and his wife, Cinde, had already endured a major medical trauma with their younger son, Earl, who had needed surgery for spina bifida, a malformation of the spinal cord and surrounding bones. In 1997 Gordon, their older son, began to exhibit some mysterious symptoms, which culminated in his being diagnosed with a brain tumor the size of a golf ball. This diagnosis led to a series of extremely trying therapies. Chemotherapy and radiation both cause pain and nausea. The combination of therapies caused Gordon to become depressed, withdrawn, and listless. His weight dropped so far that doctors administered a feeding tube. Eventually, however, the treatments worked and Gordon's ordeal came to a successful conclusion.

Steve Pettey and his wife, Cinde, are both oboists with the Dallas Wind Symphony.

Looking back, Gordon's symptoms began on Christmas eve of '96. Unexplained nausea and vomiting. It was during flu season of course and we just sort of dismissed it at that. Over the next few months it occurred off and on, but gradually becoming more frequent. We thought that maybe he had some sort of food allergy, so we tried dealing with it from that angle. Nothing ever added up. We took him to a pediatric gastroenterologist in April. She couldn't explain it either. Maybe it was something he would outgrow. On May 7th of that year [1997], our investigation of Gordon's problem was put on hold for a while when I had a serious injury to my right hand while working in my garage. Being a musician (woodwinds),

Steve Pettey, "Gordon's Cancer Story," https://home.swbell.net/pettey/index.html, February 2, 2003. Reproduced by permission of the author.

it should have ended my playing career, but with a lot of hard work and hand therapy I was back playing in about 2 months. . . .

Crisis Hits

In August, I was getting ready to go back to working again playing in the pit orchestra for the Dallas Summer Musicals. I would be playing a six week run of Disney's *Beauty and the Beast.*

It was late afternoon August 26th that things took a sudden turn. While we were having a picnic in a nearby park with Cinde's sister's family, my daughter came out of a wooded area that the kids were playing in and said that Gordon had fallen and didn't seem able to get up. When he got to his feet he was very unsteady and began to throw up again. He also said his head ached (his head had not hit the ground). I brought him back to the house and did a very quick search on the internet. All you have to do is plug in the words "headache" and "vomiting" and suddenly all links point to brain tumors. We made an appointment with our pediatrician for the next day. She (Dr. Piga) gave him a quick neurological test and immediately scheduled a CT [computed tomography] scan for him over at the hospital in Plano [Texas] later that day. I went on home and my wife Cinde took him for the scan after school. Before she had gotten back home, Dr. Piga had already called to tell me that Gordon had a brain tumor and that she had already made an appointment for the next day with a Dr. Shapiro at Children's Medical Center in Dallas. I said, "Oh, we know Dr. Shapiro already." He was Earl's (our youngest son) surgeon when he had his first shunt put in after his Spina Bifida surgery. Yes, apparently we have a "family pediatric neurosurgeon". Pretty bizarre. By now you have probably figured out that we are not unfamiliar with bad luck, however we knew we would be in good hands.

Tumor Located

At the appointment, Dr. Shapiro was surprised to see Gordon sitting up and alert based on what he had seen in the scan. It was a golf ball sized tumor in the fourth ventricle of Gordon's brain. Gordon didn't seem too concerned and was busy building with the legos in Dr. Shapiro's office. Dr. Shapiro ordered an MRI [magnetic resonance imaging] for a better look at the tumor and wrote a prescription for decadron (a steroid to reduce the cranial pressure) and scheduled the surgery for September 3rd. I arranged for someone to sub for me at the dress rehearsal for the show since that was surgery day (the show must go on . . .).

Time in a surgical waiting room passes about a thousand times slower than normal. After about 4 hours (actual) time, Dr. Shapiro came in and said he had been able to remove most of the tumor but didn't want to hurt him by taking a chance in the area of the brain stem. He said "that was a big tumor". He looked like he could use a break. We probably looked like we could use some Gatorade ourselves. He would talk to us again after the biopsy had been done.

Cinde spent the next week "living" at the ICU [intensive care unit]. I would play the show and then show up at the ICU at about 11:30 pm dressed in black (probably looking like the grim reaper) to visit them. On the last day in the ICU Dr. Winick came in to meet me and discuss treatment. The treatment protocol she described would begin with three rounds of [cancer drugs] cisplatin and etoposide, then 6 weeks of radiation followed by 9 rounds of [chemotheraphy drugs] cyclophosphamide and vincristine. It would take about a year depending on complications. I kept waiting to wake up. No such luck.

Since Gordon had been in the ICU so long, he was only in a regular room for one afternoon. It was long enough however for Dr. Shapiro to come by with confirmation of the diagnosis. Medulloblastoma with glial differentiation [a highly malignant brain tumor]. He was not upbeat about this at all. It had all sunk in by then and I knew we were in for a long haul. We had done more research than was probably good for us at that point and pretty much knew the prognosis. . . .

Chemo and Radiation Therapy

The first three rounds of chemo began on September 24th [1997]. These were three day hospital stays at 3 week intervals. He had a portacath put in under the skin on his ribs before the second round by Dr. Megason since he would become a human pincushion otherwise over the course of the year. These are incredible little devices that make putting in an IV a snap. The skin is numbed with emla cream, cleaned with betadine and alcohol and then the special needle is inserted and taped down. No pain at all. You're then ready to hook up to the "poison on tap", or blood cells, or platelets, or whatever is needed and away you go.

The nausea associated with cisplatin is legendary even with the anti-emetic, Zofran [a medicine that prevents vomitting]. Another side effect can be hearing loss, but as of yet he has had no problems in this area.

The good part about this phase was that he had not yet had the radiation treatments and his blood cell counts did not get so low as to require any blood or platelet transfusions.

Radiation treatments began on December 2nd, every weekday for 6 weeks at St. Paul medical center which is only a couple of blocks from Children's. He did get Christmas off. He had been taking phenergan for nausea during these treatments, but we switched over to Zofran due to changes in his mood that the phenergan seemed to be causing. He had become very "dark" and depressed. Taking away the phenergan helped.

The first good news of the year was when Gordon learned that he would be getting a wish from Make-a-Wish. Dr. Winick even suggested that he ask for a computer and to be very specific about it! Probably the high point of that year was the December 6th Adolphus parade when he got to ride with "Air Bud" and Ashley O'Rear [a child also fighting cancer] (of course he was only 10 at the time and probably more impressed with a dog than a girl!). We got a bit of the dog hair off his coat and taped it to a piece of cardboard for his scrapbook. Cinde said she felt like an idiot that day since she forgot the camera.

Beginning to Recover

Moving along, here is an excerpt from [a] letter we wrote April 29th, 1998: Gordon finished his radiation treatments in January. He had thirty sessions to his brain and spine. He was on a steroid during radiation which helped him feel good most of the time and made him very hungry. He gained over 15 pounds in 6 weeks. A month after radiation ended, he was phased off the steroid and chemotherapy with different drugs resumed. Immediately he became anorexic and ate almost nothing for the next 6 weeks, losing all the weight he had gained. A week after the first of the next 9 chemotherapy treatments with the drugs vincristine and cyclophosphamide, he had to go back into the hospital due to very low blood counts. He received platelets and red blood cell transfusions, antibiotics, and was started on a drug called G-CSF (or neupogen) to stimulate white blood cell production, His chemotherapy treatments are 4 weeks apart, and a week after his March treatment he had to go back in again for low blood counts, severe abdominal pain, and malnutrition/dehydration, since he was not eating. He was treated with morphine for pain, plus transfusions, antibiotics, and TPN [total parenteral nutrition] and lipids for nutrition, plus started on a NG [nasogastric; i.e. through the nose into the stomach] feeding tube. The tube has really helped him a lot. He has gotten back up to normal weight and feels much better most of the time. He still had severe abdominal pain after his chemotherapy treatment in April, and spent a few days in the hospital, but got over it quicker and did not require any transfusions or antibiotics this time. Steve is giving him G-CSF shots at home after chemotherapy, and occasionally has to reinsert the NG tube when it is thrown up. The good news is that a MRI done in February [1998] showed no sign of the tumor. He has another MRI scheduled in May and will have them every 3 months for the next couple of years, Although he has spent 29 days in the hospital since February, he is keeping up in school and will have no trouble finishing 4th grade.

There were many more transfusions of red blood cells and platelets (14 in all) over the remainder of the treatments, G-CSF shots after every round, and a pretty bad scare with blood infection. When the doctor says "this is the strongest antibiotic known", it doesn't put you at ease! We were able to give him the IV [intravenous] antibiotics at home through the portacath, fortunately.

Amusing Details

(Lawyers stop reading here!)

Let me state again here that the doctors and nurses at Children's are the best anywhere and I always have and will trust them with my children's lives. No harm came from either of these instances. Everybody is human and I wouldn't have it any other way.

If you don't count his being "dropped" during his initial surgery while he was mounted in the carriage used to position him (there is an interesting little dent in his skull—they stitched the injury and did an Xray just to be sure), there was only one other mishap in his treatment. He was doing his math homework (mean parents!) while he was receiving one of his chemos and the nurse brought in the Zofran and injected it into his IV. It wasn't Zofran however. He said that he itched and he was having trouble seeing his homework (his nose was about a half inch from the paper!). Then he said, "Daddy, I feel great! I haven't felt this good in a long time!" At this point I realized that I should probably call the nurse. She had already figured out what she had done by then however, and the staff was already wheeling in heart and respiration monitors and such. The doctor on call said that he had been given a pretty good sized dose of methadone [a heroin substitute] instead of Zofran and that the monitors were just a precaution and that it would wear off in a few hours. Gordon of course had his Make-a-Wish laptop with him and was logged on to the internet while all this discussion was going on. He had already done a search on methadone and immediately corrected the doctor saying, "No, it says here that it lasts up to 12 hours." She said, The pharmacist said that "it is usually just a few hours". ("smart-assed kid" was probably what she was thinking, though!) You'll notice that I didn't name any names but don't worry, nobody got sued. I think Gordon had earned his "buzz" by then anyhow. . . .

Life After Chemo

After the treatments were concluded and his blood counts had returned to normal levels, there were no more weekly trips to the hospital for blood tests and his checkups would occur at the comprehensive clinics (where all the doctors involved in the treatment are present). These occur a few days after each MRI. MRIs then occurred at 3 month intervals for 2 years. Gordon is now on a 6 month interval and still doing well. He has to keep taking daily doses of megestrol as an aid to his appetite which never returned. He has been giving himself growth hormone injections 6 days a week for over a year and a half now. They are working quite well. Since he had just turned 10 when the treatments began, that is when he stopped growing. Although he is 14 now, his physical age is only about that of a 12 year old. . . .

Very little of Gordon's hair has returned. We try to keep what is there quite short to keep it from looking too strange. He doesn't seem to care at all, however.

Finding Faith While Cancer Spreads

Alicia Parlette

In the following selection, Alicia Parlette, a young woman with her whole life before her, writes about discovering that she has a rare and deadly cancer. When Parlette gets her diagnosis, the news devastates her. It is all the more difficult to accept because she has already lost her mother to cancer. In gripping detail, Parlette describes the agonies of going through various scans, only to learn more discouraging news about her cancer. It has spread to her lungs and breasts. However, with the help of her boyfriend, father, stepmother, and friends, she finds the courage to accept her situation, and even to put it in a positive perspective.

Alicia Parlette is a journalist and cancer survivor. As of March 2007 her essays on living with cancer continue to be published in the San Francisco Chronicle, *where she is a staff writer.*

On March 2, [2005], I found out I have cancer. I was 23 and on my own in San Francisco, working at [the *San Francisco*] *Chronicle* as part of a two-year fellowship. I had wanted to be a journalist since fourth grade, and I had wanted to work at the *Chronicle* for almost as long. I was working as an editor, but for a few months I had felt unsettled about that decision. I wanted to do something more creative. Like write.

I was also trying to get comfortable with life. Three years earlier, my mom had died of cancer, and I was still learning how to live without her.

I came into the Chronicle Building early, at 8 a.m., because it was a Wednesday, deadline day for my department, the Friday section. It was almost 10 o'clock when I grabbed a muffin and some yogurt from the coffee shop downstairs.

I hadn't had time to take a bite when the phone rang.

For once, I didn't look at the number. I just assumed it was someone calling me back about a question I had with a story. On deadline, of course.

"Chronicle. This is Alicia."

"Hi, Alicia, this is Dr. Feldman."

Gary Feldman is my primary care doctor. I wondered why he was calling. Bad news didn't even occur to me. I was too busy for bad news. And bad news doesn't come when you're at work.

"Oh, hi, Dr. Feldman, how are you?"

"I'm fine. . . . I'm fine. Listen, we just got your pathology report back from Stanford from your breast biopsy. They're calling it alveolar soft part sarcoma."

I froze. I had no idea what that meant. I didn't even know how to spell it. Things you can't begin to spell are never good.

Medical Jargon

Dr. Feldman was still talking, but I couldn't understand anything, until I heard him say, ". . .so it's cause for concern."

"Wait, wait, hold on. I'm not any kind of medical person, so you're going to have to explain. We're talking about cancer, right? Sarcoma is a kind of cancer?"

"Yes, that's right."

I was going to throw up. I started wriggling in my chair, and I wanted to get off the phone, but he was still talking. He told me that I needed a PET [positron emission tomography] scan to determine whether it had spread and that I could probably get one on Friday. Then I'd need another CT [computed tomography] scan of my lungs.

My lungs. A year before, when I'd had a bad cough, scans had shown spots on my lungs, but nothing had come of it. In November, I found a lump in my right breast, and on Feb. 15, it was removed—a lumpectomy—for a biopsy. All of a sudden, every bad feeling I'd ever had, every fear that lurked in the back of my brain, seemed to be coming true. The words I'd heard from earlier doctors whispered behind Dr. Feldman's voice:

"You're healthy."

"It's usually nothing."

"You're too young."

All of the nice things the doctors and nurses had said to me now seemed cruel. Dr. Feldman finished. "So I'll get you set up for that PET scan and call you back, OK?" I hung up the phone and sat at my desk. I felt the weight of his words being shoved down my throat, and I felt my mouth thicken.

I stared at my screen for a few minutes—two, five, more, I have no idea. I tried to read the story on my computer, but the words didn't make sense. Oh, God, now I couldn't read.

I looked to my right, to my friend Bernadette, but she was on the phone. I looked to my left, to Jan, but her back was to me, and walking two steps over to her seemed too much effort, like I would collapse before I could take a step.

Bernadette was off the phone. But now she was standing up. She was walking away. I knew I had to tell someone, but I couldn't speak. Tears were choking me.

I stared at my computer. I was thinking about talking, but I couldn't even say hi. I tried looking at the picture of my dog, Tasha, and couldn't. It would make me cry.

Remembering Mother's Fate

I could feel pressure building in my head. My shoulders ached from tension, and I knew I would give myself a headache if I didn't let go and cry. But I wasn't going to just cry uncontrollably at my desk, so I told myself I had to get to the bathroom. "Stand up and go," I thought, and I was on my feet, holding onto cubicle walls as I walked past my desk, other people's desks.

Luckily, there was no one in the bathroom. I went into the third stall, thinking, "This is my favorite stall. This is good." I shut the door, locked it with shaking hands and fell to my knees. I thought I was going to throw up, but instead I spat twice and tears started dripping into the toilet bowl.

I was thinking of my mom, Pam, of how similar this felt to the night she died, when I saw her eyes glaze over and I fell to the hospital floor. And it reminded me of a year after her death, that night when I was working as a summer intern at the *Sacramento Bee,* when her death finally sank in. I had made at least five trips to the bathroom to pull it together, kneel on the floor and pray.

But now I couldn't even pray. Too many thoughts were running through my head, and I couldn't decipher anything. I could feel each thought pounding to get out, banging against my skull. It hurt. . . .

Undergoing A Scan

Thursday morning, my boyfriend, John, came to Concord from Reno, where we had graduated from the University of Nevada. It wasn't a whole lot of quality time, since I was on the phone to doctors or schedulers or friends or family members so much that he and Sally eventually cut me off and wouldn't let me pick up my cell phone, but things felt more normal with him around.

On Friday, John and I met my best friend, Ashley, and her mom, Pat, to go to San Francisco for my PET scan (which I found out stood for positron emission tomography). Pat and her husband met my parents when I was an infant and Pat was pregnant with Ashley.

Ashley and I grew up calling each other's mother Mommy Pat and Mommy Pam, and we still do. At my mom's funeral, Ashley read my eulogy for me. Being around them feels like being with family because, to me, they are family.

Pat drove cautiously from her home in Moraga to San Francisco, navigating the city's hills with the help of John's directions and my random shouts of advice from the backseat.

She seemed surprised, but thankful, that we got there and ushered us into the elevator so I wouldn't be late.

I don't know why, but I was excited about this appointment. I was in a good mood from hanging out with Ashley, Pat and John, and it felt like a reprieve from work and my teary phone calls. We settled into a leather couch to watch TV and read magazines. I was relaxed, ready to see what a PET scan was all about.

Having a PET scan means a technician fills you with radioactivity so a big doughnut-looking machine can take pictures of your entire body to see where the cancer has spread. To get radioactive, you are injected with radioactive-tagged sugar water.

Fear of Needles

I confess: I am terrified of needles. I know almost everyone has some kind of aversion to them. It makes no sense to have metal shoved into the body, let alone the veins. And every time I tell some tech or nurse or doctor this, they just smile and nod. "We'd be worried if you liked it," they say.

But every time that needle appears, I start crying and hyperventilating, and the techs don't know what to do with me. So with the PET scan, the same thing happened. "I just get so worked up," I told the tech. "It's in my head, I know, but I just don't like needles"—tourniquet is snapped on—"and I don't like the feel of the blood trapped in my hand"—alcohol is rubbed on my skin—"and I know I make it worse than it is—Owwww!"

I spent an hour waiting for the radioactivity to spread through my body. While John and I sat and watched *My Cousin Vinny* on TV, I convinced myself I could feel the radioactivity, like it was seeking out the cancer and readying for reconnaissance. "Thisaway, boys! Onward—to the lungs!"

In the PET-scan room, I had to lie on my back in the middle of the big, plastic doughnut for almost an hour without moving. To their credit, the operators of the imaging studio piped in some whimsical harp music, so it felt more like a yoga session than a medical scan. Without the yoga.

Around minute 37, my bladder got antsy. I tried to shift my weight to get relief, but that's hard to do when you're not allowed to move. Suddenly, I felt claustrophobic. Had my doughnut bed always been this small? What were those noises above my head? And where the hell was the technician?

A little later, she walked in. "How's it going?" she asked.

"Oh, fine, fine," I said. "There's just one little thing—I sort of have to go to the bathroom. Would that be possible to do anytime soon?"

"Oh, no, I don't think so. Unless it's an emergency."

"Nope, nope, not an emergency." My bladder was threatening to explode, and there I was, being polite. "About how much longer?"

"Oh, I don't know, 15 minutes or so."

The rest of the scan passed in embarrassed discomfort. . . .

Discouraging Results

On Tuesday—the day John was going back to Reno, the day before I would go back to work—I heard bad news from Dr. Feldman.

The scans showed the cancer had spread.

It was in my lungs and around my right hip. Well, actually, it was in my "right gluteal region," a nice way of talking about my butt.

I Had Butt Cancer

But before I could laugh much about that, I thought of something. Something devastating. When I was 16, I ran cross-country. I have never been athletic, but running came naturally, I loved it. I liked going to practice, being in shape, pushing myself and sprinting that last leg to the finish line.

147

But after only one season, I started having pains in my hip. Every time I stopped running, pain shot down the front of my right leg, and my hip ached.

After meeting with a sports orthopedist and getting an MRI that showed a spot near my hip, my parents and I went to UCSF to see a specialist. My mom was a wreck. This was about six months before her diagnosis, and the idea of cancer seemed so alien.

We didn't have to worry for long. The specialist said it was a hemangioma—a benign cluster of blood vessels. "It can never turn into cancer," he said. "It's nothing to worry about. You'll have to stop running, but you won't have surgery. Stick to low-impact sports and you'll be fine."

My mom was thrilled, but I was devastated. No running? I had found a sport I was actually good at, and already it was taken from me. I yelled at her in the car on the way home. 'Mom, why are you so happy? I can't run! I can't run ever again! I'd rather have cancer and have them just take it out! At least I could run!

A Missed Opportunity

Talking to my doctor seven years later, I felt guilty about those words. He said it looked like a mass in my right hip was the source of the cancer. The hemangioma might not have been a hemangioma, but a tumor hiding within my veins. Not an egregious misdiagnosis, I thought at first, but pretty horrible considering that the cancer had, during those years, spread to my lungs and my breast.

Doctors later told me that the cancer might have looked so much like a hemangioma that the two were indistinguishable on an MRI. Or that it could have been a hemangioma, and then a cancer grew underneath. I didn't believe that for a second.

While I was talking to Dr. Feldman, I was relieved to find out the cancer hadn't spread to places I hadn't already been worrying about. It could have been in my stomach, in my uterus. But instead, it was only in places that were already suspicious: my breast, my lungs, my butt.

Oh, butt cancer. Always good for a laugh. . . .

Two days later, I sat in the UCSF Comprehensive Cancer Center, feeling overwhelmed. Dr. Feldman had recommended that I see an orthopedic oncologist, because of my hip, and so there I was in an examination room, waiting with my dad; Sally; and Chris, my stepmom. My dad had remarried in September, and Chris really wanted to be at the appointment to support me.

My dad was swiveling around on the doctor's stool; Chris sat, pen and paper in hand, in a chair across from him; Sally was next to me, holding my hand and patting my leg; and I sat on the examining table, legs dangling and palms sweating. Four of us in that room made it hard to breathe. I wanted out.

To calm down, I took in the details. The way my dad's hair was combed. What kind of pen Chris had. How often Sally looked up at me, smiling.

When the doctor came in, I started focusing on the room. The mauve curtain. The computer in the corner. The crunchiness of my gown. He sat there calculating how rare my cancer was ("Let's see . . . uh . . . huh . . . 1 percent of. . .right. . .and-. . .well. . .1 in 50 million, maybe?") and the limited options I had ("We usually don't use chemotherapy because it doesn't work, but you'll have to talk to someone else about that"), and I felt myself weaving in and out of panic. One second I felt like I was going to pass out; the next, I focused on his gray-blue tie. The details seemed increasingly important.

Gaining Perspective

I was set up to see other doctors and with a plan to meet again, but no treatment. No concrete options. I noticed myself stepping back and thinking of it as a play, not my life. This was too horrific to be my life.

As I sat there, I could feel myself detach. And in that moment I thought, "What a great story this will make."

That's when I knew I was a writer. When things were more frightening than I could ever imagine and my tiny little existence was spinning and careening out of control, my first reaction was to think about recasting it as a drama, as a struggle, as a way to share my little existence that didn't seem so little anymore.

I am still in awe of the way life's puzzles fall into place. I think this is because, right now, God is giving me a bigger look at how the jigsaw is mapped out. Not much bigger, but big enough for me to see that even tragedies are linked with blessings, and that among my many blessings is the chance to write my story. Right at the time when my world is upended— and right at a time when I'm aching to be more creative, to find an outlet, to finally write—God practically drops this opportunity in my lap.

If I get through this, this story will help me remember the important moments along the way, the details, the dizzying emotions. And, in the worst of all circumstances, if I go through this life-changing ordeal and my body just wears out and I die, I will die a writer. The one thing I've always wanted to be.

Surviving Non-Hodgkins Lymphoma

Jonathan Alter

In the midst of a presidential campaign, a political reporter gets an unexpected call. Tests show that the source of his stomach pain is a large tumor. So began journalist Jonathan Alter's struggle with non-Hodgkins lymphoma (NHL), a form of cancer that works its way through the body's network of lymph nodes. In the following selection he describes how he became one of more than 10 million American cancer survivors. Following his diagnosis, Alter went into a profound depression, and could only find relief from what he calls a mental hell in his work. The more he learned about his cancer, the worse he felt. He had a rare variety of NHL that is particularly aggressive. Alter was fortunate, however, to have access to some of the best cancer doctors and treatments available, and following chemotherapy and a bone marrow transplant, he made a comeback. He has been in remission for several years and is able to continue his journalistic career.

Alter is a senior editor for Newsweek *magazine. His political columns and coverage are widely praised. He is also a contributing correspondent and commentator for NBC News.*

I took the call on my cell phone at the Starbucks in New York's Penn Station. It was from a doctor I barely knew telling me that a CT scan—ordered after three weeks of worsening stomach pain—showed a large mass in my abdomen, with what she said was "considerable lymph node involvement." I rubbed my eyes and sensed the truth instantly: cancer, and not one that had been detected early. I was 46 years old and had not spent a night in the hospital since I was born. Nonsmoker. No junk food beyond the occasional barbecue potato chips. Jogged a couple of times a week. I was not remotely ready for this.

It was Super Tuesday, March 2, 2004, the day voters would select most of the delegates to the Democratic National Convention. Although the complete diagnosis was still several days off, the intense abdominal pain meant that my wife, Emily, and I had no time to stop, absorb and adjust to our twisted new world. We immediately began negotiating the endless round of doctors' appointments and insurance hassles that mark a cancer patient's life. With my head on fire, I quietly endured a festive lunch with political reporters and anchors, then went back to work. My job that day was to analyze the end of John Edwards's presidential campaign.

Hanging On

Three years later [2007], I'm in remission and, strangely enough, thinking once more about the future of Edwards and his family. Like the 10.5 million other cancer survivors in the United States, I experienced a bit of extra stress last week. When Elizabeth Edwards's [John's wife] breast cancer recurred in her bones and Tony Snow's colon cancer recurred in his liver, the cold fear that many of us live with every day crept a little closer. The good news is that the candor of Edwards and Snow (who is recuperating from surgery but has been open about his situation from his perch as White House press secretary) has helped stimulate a useful national conversation about how people handle a cancer diagnosis. It has also exposed the foolishness of a few busybodies who don't have cancer, but feel free to judge the complex choices made by those who do.

My own story isn't typical, because none is. Every patient reacts a little differently, both biologically and psychologically. The only constant in cancer is inconstancy; the only certainty is a future of uncertainty, a truism for all of modern life but one made vivid by life-threatening illness. According to the latest projections, a third of all Americans will be diagnosed with cancer at some point during their lifetimes, most likely when they're old. Many will never achieve remission at all, while the lucky ones like me get to live with a sword of Damocles hanging over our heads. A friend compares his semiannual scans to visiting a parole officer. When the scans are clean, it's worth another six months of freedom, though with no guarantee of extra time for good behavior.

In my case, the news went from bad to worse. To calm my nerves before the laparoscopic surgery (they cut my colon into a semicolon and removed my appendix while they were at it), I heard some happy talk about how the bowel obstruction might be benign. As I recovered and watched the slow gait of my internist down the hospital corridor I knew otherwise. "Time is an illusion," he told me cryptically, explaining that after a certain age, a few years could seem like many, and many could seem like few. I was informed that I had non-Hodgkin's lymphoma, a blood cancer that would likely shorten my life without ending it any time soon.

But we didn't yet know the all-important cell type. The day after being discharged, I grew impatient with the slowness of the pathology report and had the hospital lab fax it to me directly. Big mistake. After Googling "mantle cell lymphoma," I learned it was a rare and nasty form of the disease with a terrifying prognosis.

Mental Agony

By this time I was in mental free fall. Friends later said I handled it courageously, but they were wrong. American culture rewards cheerful stoicism, a quality that cancer patients usually display in public but find difficult to sustain in private, especially at the beginning. I collapsed in tears only briefly, but retreated into a fog of unshakable misery. My detachment alarmed Emily, who wisely resisted many well-intentioned efforts by family and friends to coddle me. She understood that their instinct to be protective was making me into a weaker person than I needed to be. So she lovingly but firmly pushed me back into some semblance of normal life. "Get off the Internet and get back to your real work!" she insisted on more than one occasion.

I slept only with the help of sleeping pills. After taking too many, I botched the disclosure of my condition to our three kids, then ages 14, 12 and 10, stumbling so badly over my words that Emily finally sent me to bed. Our family freely discusses everything but in this case we only told them the extent of the problem when we had a plan in place to try to fix it. They didn't want to know the details, and their self-protective lack of curiosity on this subject (and this subject alone) was a relief to me. We rarely talked about it with them thereafter, an unfashionable approach I would recommend. Physically, I felt OK; emotionally, I was in hell. A woman I knew who was dying of breast cancer told me that none of the pain she was suffering at the end of her life compared with that first month and the daze of diagnosis.

I fell back on what I knew—reporting and analysis—and undertook a furious round of investigative phone calls. Everyone agreed that it was critical to be examined at a major cancer center, where doctors would have seen my disease much more often than at other hospitals. (I was even told of studies showing the farther one travels for treatment, the better the chance of survival.) With the help of friends, I finally got an appointment at New York's Memorial Sloan-Kettering Cancer Center. It happened on my wife's birthday, the only present she wanted.

The Worst Confirmed

After receiving a second opinion on the lab results, the brilliant doctor who became my oncologist administered an excruciating bone-marrow biopsy, which felt as if I were on a medieval rack. The results confirmed that I was Stage Four, the most advanced, though the systemic nature of lymphoma may have made that less dire than in other cancers. He told me that my two-year odds of survival were essentially a coin toss, and that my best chance to improve them lay in four months of accelerated chemotherapy, followed by a bone-marrow transplant, an aggressive regimen previously used mostly for relapsed patients.

Many patients place full trust in their physician and never second-guess them. I was constitutionally incapable of that, so I hit him with a barrage of questions. Why this chemo protocol and not another used by a different hospital? Why not enroll me in a clinical trial? Why couldn't he tell me more? Even though I admired him, I continued reporting. With no standard of care for this disease, each expert I managed to get on the phone had a slightly different take on how it should be treated, which I later discovered is common with cancer.

I vacuumed up everything I could. (Cancer is unbelievably complex: lymphoma alone is made up of more than 30 different types.) I even became capable of decoding some of the doctors' medical jargon, which is like picking up a foreign language. The more I knew, the more frustrated I grew at the Catch-22 of oncology, which is that the most cutting-edge therapies are used only for the sickest patients, when it's often too late. Newly diagnosed patients get the old stuff, unless they get much sicker, when it's often too late for them, too.

But a little knowledge can be a dangerous and depressing thing. The Internet is a fantastic resource for patients, who increasingly use it to ask pertinent questions of their doctors. It can also baffle and disorient. Some of what I read about mantle cell lymphoma was out of date or even wrong, and logging on began to make me feel anxious. I thought Emily was in denial and she thought I was an easy mark for every cancer "cure." We quarreled about it. When I tasted the rank "noni juice" I'd ordered on the Internet, I knew she was right.

Going Public

One Web resource, however, was indispensable. My sister set up an account with a nonprofit site called caringbridge.org that brought order and even pleasure to my communication with the outside world. Instead of having to repeat my story endlessly on the phone or in individual e-mails, I could offer periodic updates, then watch in amazement and gratitude as the good wishes, parodies and embarrassing stories about me from fourth grade rolled in. The site kept practically everyone in my universe informed while easing their sense of helplessness—and mine. The postings of my children and my mother-in-law became particular crowd-pleasers and before long the idea spread through parts of the media world. Even B.D. from "Doonesbury," home from Iraq and hospitalized at Walter Reed, got a caringbridge site.

I decided early not to keep my cancer a secret. I felt enough stress already without trying to figure out who knew and who didn't. One morning on the radio, [broadcaster] Don Imus, sensing something in my voice, asked in his inimitable way why I sounded awful. I blurted out to a few million listeners that I was headed for chemo that day. But I kept the prognosis under wraps for fear that people would pity me or write me off. By then I knew that for all the new openness about cancer, sick people still get sidelined.

The idea of joining a support group held no appeal for me, in part because my disease is so rare and I had little interest in hearing about other kinds of cancer. ("My sister-in-law's cousin had prostate cancer and he's doing fine," I was once told, unhelpfully.) But we mantle cell survivors found each other by phone and e-mail. Unfortunately, many hospitals still do little or nothing to connect newly diagnosed patients with those who have survived the same disease for several years, though this is what we crave.

Support from Others

Most people I know—and many I don't—were unbelievably supportive, offering prayers and comfort when I needed it most. I can't even conceive how people without close family (my brother even shaved his head in solidarity), friends and co-workers can survive the ordeal. Millions of Americans live alone and fight the disease mostly alone. They are the heroic ones.

The experience changes your relationship with friends, as some who were once mere acquaintances step up magnificently and others who were closer fade away. The long faces and doleful "How are you, *really*?" false intimacies were less welcome than the cheerful ribbing and sense I was being viewed normally. Emily and I got a laugh out of those people so interested in my initial symptoms that we concluded the inquiries into my health were more about them and whether the indigestion they were experiencing might be cancer. Others just wanted to know whether I had "beaten" it so they could check me off as one less person to worry about. Even now, it's just inaccurate to say that I have.

As my chemotherapy continued through the spring, my spirits lifted a bit. One of the worst parts of cancer is the loss of control, the sense that you have no recourse when your body betrays you. That's why nutrition and hygiene became so important to me in that period. For the first time, I actually understood how someone could develop an obsessive-compulsive disorder involving repeated handwashing. My own insistence on it was beginning to drive my family nuts. But I was determined to stay free of infection when my immunity was down during treatment. Chemo brought out the warrior in me, and the obedient servant. If the doctor suggested drinking a gallon of fluids on the first day after treatment, I didn't drink three and three-quarters quarts. I drank the full gallon, for maximum control, or the illusion of it.

The Worst Passes

My luck began to turn when I found I was avoiding the worst side effects, with the help of a dozen pills a day. I suffered fatigue, bone pain, anemia, total hair loss (my family said I looked like an egg), hemorrhoids, numbness and foot cramps, but thanks to anti-nausea drugs, which I popped prophylactically at $70 a pill, no vomiting. I missed my 25th college reunion but made the 2004 Democratic convention, with syringes in my bag and a catheter in my chest that my wife nervously learned to clean and dress. Cancer tests any marriage, trying to work tiny cracks into fissures. But as I slowly checked out of my fog, ours prospered.

By this time I had fashioned my own daily recovery plan, which I dubbed *Herman*. The H stood for humor, a few minutes each day with "Curb Your Enthusiasm" or Will Ferrell or an Ian Frazier story or a friend who would make me laugh. E was—and is—for exercise, which may not fight cancer but clears my head. R represented religion. At the depths, I tried to read something about Judaism or talk to God a little every day, though like a soldier escaped from the foxhole, I've backslid since. (Religion often morphed into superstition, as I avoided the sweater I had worn on the day of a bad test result and refused, long after remission, to refer to my cancer in the past tense for fear of tempting a recurrence.) M was for meditation, which with the help of my friend Barbara helped calm me for a time. A was for attitude. Studies show no connection between a good attitude and reducing tumor size and I can't stand the way our therapeutic society makes people feel that cancer is their own fault because they weren't more chipper. But mind-set is important. By chance, I was already at work on a book about Franklin D. Roosevelt, and the writing offered a useful distraction from cancer. His upbeat attitude after being stricken with polio was inspirational for me, and made me wonder, What Would Franklin Do? N stood for niceness to my family. They bore the brunt of my irritability, which I tried to reduce, not always successfully.

Humanity and Jealousy

As I learned about myself, I also learned a lot about medicine. Most cancer doctors are awe-inspiring in their humanity and dedication. They make, say, hedge-fund billionaires (not to mention journalists) look puny and insignificant. But I also found oncology full of the same mammoth egos and petty jealousies that plague any high-powered field. Doctors from competing institutions are often so competitive that they talk to each other only a couple of times a year at conferences. They do lab work on parallel tracks instead of collaborating. And under pressure from hospital lawyers, they frequently even refuse to share cell lines with other qualified researchers, which retards progress toward cures and is clearly unethical. Thanks to a wealthy mantle cell lymphoma survivor, ours is one of the first subsets of cancer to establish a consortium to get top experts in the field to exchange ideas regularly. Every cancer should have a consortium.

And every cancer doctor would do well to recalibrate on occasion the balance he or she strikes between science and hope. While the survival odds they offer might be technically accurate (X percentage with Y cancer will survive five years), they are often misleading and sometimes unnecessarily cruel. Patients and families obsess over these survival-rate statistics, but they reduce the countless variables of a person's genetic makeup and environmental exposure to a number, which is cold and often phony. Depending on the individual (whose age is usually not even factored into the statistics), a 50 percent chance of survival could easily be 80 percent—or 20 percent. Moreover, few patients understand the meaning of the term "median survival." That simply means half live less time and half live more—perhaps much more.

Dr. Jerome Groopman, the Harvard Medical School oncologist who became my informal patient advocate (which every patient needs and few get) and later my indispensable friend, told me that he wished he had a nickel for every patient he knew who was told he had an "incurable" disease and is still doing just fine. Groopman's new best seller, *How Doctors Think*, explains the self-protective psychology behind the pessimism of so many doctors, who don't like to view the death of a patient as a comment on their abilities. So they resort to saying it's a "bad disease" or "incurable." What doctors should say—and often do—is that a particularly challenging cancer might be incurable now, but if we can keep you alive, a while longer, a cure might come, as it did for [champion cyclist] Lance Armstrong's testicular cancer. Patients need to do their part by enrolling more readily in clinical trials, which most avoid. And they should stop pressing their doctors for an exactitude that doesn't exist.

A Saving Transplant

The climax of my treatment was a bone-marrow transplant in August of 2004. There are two kinds: an allogeneic transplant—the only true cure—involves a donor. But I had no sibling match, and using an unrelated donor carries a one-third morbidity rate. Because the earlier rounds of chemo had achieved remission, I was eligible tor a less dangerous autologous transplant. I was hooked up to a machine that extracted (or "harvested") millions of my stem cells, which were then frozen. Once admitted to Sloan-Kettering for a 23-day stay, I was hit with high-dose chemotherapy, the most toxic in the chemo family. The point was to knock my white blood cell count down to zero, a process that confined me to my room for two weeks. Had I, with no immune system, wandered into the hall and caught something, I would have died. After my stem cells were defrosted and transplanted back into me, along with several other blood transfusions, my blood counts slowly increased.

For me, the experience was not as bad as advertised. Before I felt the brunt of it, I even managed to bang out a *Newsweek* column from the hospital. I avoided the horrible mouth sores and most of the other common side effects. Family and friends visited everyday, as long as they washed their hands carefully and stayed on the other side of the room. Even when I was too weak to move or say much, I enjoyed their chatter. When I got home I could walk only a few steps. But within a few weeks I was walking a mile and by Election Night 2004 I was back on TV after eight months, balder if not wiser.

The Cost of Cancer

During my *annus horribilis, Newsweek* let me work at home and helped me navigate the insanity of the American healthcare system. The claim forms are impenetrable and accompanied by pseudo-sympathetic bill collectors. How do other patients with life-threatening illnesses even begin to handle it? Cancer is seriously expensive, and no insurance company covers all of it. I met a lymphoma survivor whose wife left him after he sold the house to pay for his transplant. Now he's clinically depressed, too. But at least he's not uninsured or bankrupt. The majority of personal bankruptcies in the United States come from medical expenses, not sloth. In its hideous 2005 bankruptcy "reform," Congress sided with credit-card companies and kicked cancer survivors when they were down.

Six weeks after my transplant—and again at six months—I received additional infusions of Rituxan, one of the new, less toxic and more targeted cancer therapies. In the two years since, my checkups have consisted of colonoscopies (I've had eight altogether) and CT scans. Recently I graduated from three-month scans to six-month scans. I grow anxious before each one, of course, terrified that I will be exiled once more to the penal colony of the sick.

In between, every little ache or pain sends a jolt of dread. But I run three miles a day to stay in shape and I try to channel some of what my father has taught me about being a combat aviator in World War II, where he learned to balance fear and fatalism. At home, my children seem unaffected, insulated by the glorious narcissism of adolescence. I can even envision a time when a day finally passes without my thinking of cancer.

Serious illness has a way of crystallizing life, which is why so many people change jobs or spouses or views of the world when they fall ill. On some level, they weren't at peace with their old life and suddenly found the motivation to change it. I was happy with my old life, and all I wanted was to get it back, without having to become a professional cancer survivor or expert on coping.

In a taxi en route to lunch on that awful Super Tuesday, I experienced a powerful premonition: I have cancer, it's going to be bad, but I'll live until I'm 90. Probably not, but I turn 50 this year and, full of hope, recall that great line from [the movie] *The Shawshank Redemption*: "You can get busy living, or get busy dying." For me, it's no contest.

An Asian American Faces Breast Cancer

Susan Shinagawa

In the following selection Susan Shinagawa, an Asian American, describes her battle with breast cancer. It began when she discovered a lump in her breast during a self-exam. A cancer doctor told her not to get a biopsy, because, according to him, she was too young, she had no family history of cancer, and "Asian women don't get breast cancer." However, when she eventually got tested, it turned out that she did indeed have cancer. Worse yet, after surgery and treatment, her cancer recurred. However, she struggled on. Shinagawa describes in stark personal detail the ups and downs of her battle and her effort to advocate for herself in a system that refused to accept her situation.

Susan Shinagawa chairs the Intercultural Cancer Council, the nation's largest multicultural coalition addressing the unequal burden of cancer in minority and medically underserved communities. She lives near San Diego, California, with her husband.

I took a class on breast self-exams in 1991. I took it because a friend of mine was teaching it and she asked me to show up. That was the only reason I went, though I should have been going for my own health. I was over the age of thirty and hadn't had any kids. After the class, I was actually very diligent about doing a breast self-exam every month. Six months later, I found a lump that just kind of popped up out of nowhere. And following the instruction of my class, I followed it for two months to see if it made any changes during my menstrual cycle, and it didn't. At the time, I was about to

Susan Shinagawa, *LiveStrong: Inspirational Stories from Cancer Survivors—From Diagnosis to Treatment and Beyond.* New York: Broadway Books, 2005.

go on a personal leave of absence from work, so I thought that at the same time I was having my teeth cleaned and getting my eyes checked, I ought to have this lump checked out. So I went to see a doctor, and she looked at it and said, "Well, you know, I'm not really worried about it, but since we can feel it, let's go get a mammogram." It was negative. But because it was palpable, meaning we could feel it, the diagnostic radiologist said, "Well, let's do a sonogram." So we did a sonogram and she found that it was a solid mass. So she in turn sent me to see a cancer surgeon. He examined my breast and looked at the negative mammogram. We talked about my family history. And he said to me, "Susan, I don't think you have anything to worry about. You're too young to have breast cancer. You have no family history of cancer. And besides, Asian women don't get breast cancer." So I'm thinking this is what you want to hear when you're young. You don't want to have breast cancer. But I got home that night and I kept thinking. I really do believe in women's intuition, and this little voice in my head was telling me there was something wrong here. The doctor had said that if I lowered my intake of caffeine, the lumps would go away. And I wrote him a note that night that said, "I don't drink coffee. I don't drink tea. I don't drink sodas. I don't like chocolate. I don't take aspirin because I don't like to swallow pills. And I really don't think I can lower my intake of caffeine anymore. Won't you please do a biopsy? I'm about to go on a personal leave of absence. And while I have insurance, it'd be nice to get it done." He found me in the hall the next day at the medical center and said, "Susan, you have to trust me. I see thousands of young women like you every year, and you do not have breast cancer. And I absolutely refuse to do a biopsy." So I'm thinking to myself again, "Okay. He's the expert."

Medical Disbelief

I went on my personal leave of absence. But then there was another thing about my lump. It hurt. In 1991, the belief in the medical community was that if you had a breast lump and it hurt, there was no way it could be cancer, because breast cancer doesn't hurt. So a lot of people were telling me, "You're just being paranoid. Don't worry about it. You're just thinking about it, because you're doing these breast self-exams." But the pain kept it in the forefront of my mind. So, two months later, I decided I was going to get a second opinion. And I went to another university medical center, where they conducted clinical cancer trials, and saw another surgeon. He looked at my films and he did an exam and said that he agreed with the first surgeon that he didn't think I had anything to worry about. In fact, he said, "I could tell you with 99.9 percent accuracy that you do not have breast cancer." Well, of course, I had already decided that I was not going to take no for an answer, so I told him that I wanted to be 100 percent sure. I wanted the biopsy. So he did an incisional biopsy a couple of days later. I was awake for the surgery. I was just under a local anesthetic. So he asked me if I wanted to see the lump, and I said, "Yes." So he brought it over and showed it to me, said, "Absolutely, you don't have anything to worry about. This is definitely not a cancer." And I asked him how he knew, and he said that there was so much fat growing around the lump that it had to have been there at least ten years, and he was very sure it wasn't a breast cancer. "Go home. Live a happy life." So I went home, had breakfast. I was delighted.

Positive Diagnosis

Next day, I get a phone call. I had actually been out looking for a job and I came home about five-thirty. There was a message on the answering machine from the surgeon telling me, "Susan, please call me at this number. And if you can't reach me there, call me at this number. And if you can't reach me there, page me at this number." I was pretty sure that he didn't have good news for me, since he insisted that I find him. And, of course, when I called him, he said, "Susan, I'm very sorry to tell you, but you have breast cancer." He was very shocked.

He told me that when he got the call from the pathology lab that he was quite certain that they had switched my specimen with somebody else's. He actually walked to the lab to check for himself.

I totally freaked out. My first reaction was, "Oh, my god, I've got breast cancer. I'm going to die a horrible death!" And then I thought, "Oh, my god, I've got breast cancer. It's going to be really bad. I'm going to commit suicide." And then I thought. "Oh, my god, I've got breast cancer. I'd better do something about it." I'm sure these thoughts went through my head in a matter of seconds, but I very clearly remember having them. I worked at a medical center. I didn't know a lot about cancer, but I was intelligent and educated. But still I had this knee-jerk reaction. It really surprised me that I reacted that way. But I very soon decided that I was going to do something about it.

I ended up speaking to a woman who I had met right before I left my job at the medical center to go on my leave. She had just started working there as a patient ombudsman for the cancer center. The only thing I knew about her was that she was about my age and had had cancer. So I got her phone number, called her up, and left a message for her. She called me back a day later, and we talked on the phone for about an hour and a half. And after that conversation, I hung up the phone and my feeling was, I can do this. I can do this. The best thing I did was talk to somebody else who had been there. It really instilled confidence in me that this was going to be a challenge, but not a problem.

Self-Education

I went to the library and checked out about fourteen books, which I read in two days. I wanted to know as much about what I was dealing with as I possibly could. I read a lot about statistics. It's kind of a trap that you fall into as a patient, because you think you want to know the statistics. But you learn later on that statistics really don't mean anything, because when it comes to you, it's always 100 percent. Still, the statistics are very alluring. What is the chance of the breast cancer coming back? What's my chance that I'm going to die? What's my chance that I'm going to live? I figured that at the age of thirty-four and having a premenopausal breast cancer, the risk of the breast cancer coming back sometime throughout my life was probably about 30 percent. But I didn't want to have to worry about this. And I had small breasts. I never identified myself by my breasts. I think in American society, we're kind of socialized to think that breasts are the be-all-end-all physical attribute. Well, that wasn't the way it was for me. So I didn't care about whether or not I kept it. What I did care about was not having to worry about this 30 percent chance of this cancer coming back. So I decided to have a mastectomy. It was an informed decision that I made on my own. I really thought hard about it.

After that I wanted to follow up my surgery with adjuvant chemotherapy. I was told by a number of oncologists that I was just being hysterical and paranoid. But I was not going to take no for an answer. I had already learned not to take no for an answer once. And so I had eight cycles of chemotherapy. I continued to do a lot of reading of the medical literature while I was in treatment. In the middle of my treatment, the first reports were just coming out saying that there was a definite significant survival advantage for premenopausal women with early-stage breast cancer who had surgery followed by adjuvant chemotherapy. I felt totally vindicated. I was surprised that all these people were telling me that I was being crazy for wanting it.

Cancer Resurfaces

I did really well with my treatment. I never thought I was going to have any problem with cancer again. One day I was home cooking dinner, and while the food was on the stove, I sat down at the couch to watch the nightly news. And I remember very specifically that I started to get this pain in my left hip. And it got worse and worse and worse through the night. I couldn't get rid of it. It was one of those pains where at first I thought it was just the position I was sitting in, but I couldn't get it to go away. And it was so bad that I couldn't sleep. The next morning I felt fine. But one week later, the exact same thing happened. Cooking dinner, sitting on the couch, looking at the television to watch the evening news, and the pain starts again, except this time, not only is it in my hip, but it's all the way down my left leg. The next day I went to work but the pain was still really bothering me. I called up my primary physician. She had me come in right away. I never went back to work after that day. She started me on a whole bunch of diagnostic tests. I was taking four and five different tests and procedures every day. Within two weeks, the entire left side of my body was either numb or weak. My foot was drooping. The left side of my face was drooping. My left retina was unresponsive. I was in a wheelchair and in a whole lot of pain. And it turns out that I was diagnosed with recurrent breast cancer, but it had appeared in my cerebral spinal fluid. Not a good thing to have.

It's funny, because this whole time my doctors were thinking about a recurrence of cancer, it never even occurred to me. Never occurred to me once. I don't know why. I guess I had always assumed that if I had a recurrence, it was going to be in the breast and it was going to be something that was really obvious to me.

This time it was a whole slew of different treatments. Before the recurrence was actually diagnosed, they had started me on a high dose of steroids. I remember the doctor telling me that I might gain a few pounds. So eighty-seven pounds later, I had surgery to have an Ommaya catheter implanted in my brain, through which I received chemotherapy every day. I also had radiation to my lumbar spine, because they had done some other test that showed there was some blockage of my cerebral spinal fluid. Every day for five weeks, I was getting radiation and chemotherapy that they would inject through the catheter in my brain. The chemo made me sicker than a dog. I'd never been so nauseated in my life. And with the radiation on top of that, because it was hitting my intestines and my stomach, made it just really horrible. At that point, I didn't want to finish treatment. It was just unbearable. But I finally got through it. After I had all the radiation and treatment, the weakness of my left side resolved itself.

Advocating for Asian Women

My advocacy work is a direct result of my experience of being diagnosed with my cancer and what I went through trying to get treatment for my cancer and my cancer pain. In the beginning, I started out speaking up about young women being diagnosed with cancer. Everyone is telling you that young women don't get breast cancer. Certainly, cancer is a disease primarily of older people. And the percentages, again, for young women who get breast cancer are small, but I think it's an absolute lie and disservice to tell young women that they don't have to worry about it. So that was the first thing I started speaking out about. And then it occurred to me, gee, how many Asian women are being told that they don't have to worry about a lump, because Asian women don't get breast cancer? So I read up on that. And what I found out is that the statistics that say young Asian women don't get breast cancer are all based on the National Cancer Institute data, which is collected nationwide. The problem with that data is that it doesn't take into account the demographics of the Asian-American population, which is about 70 percent first-generation immigrant. Asian immigrants *coming from* the Asian countries in the world have the lowest breast-cancer rates globally. So when you take that into account, what you're reporting on in the United States in terms of breast-cancer

169

rates for Asian women are the breast-cancer rates of first-generation women who come from the countries with the lowest breast-cancer rates. Those statistics don't report on someone like me who was born here. My parents were born here. I'm third-generation Japanese-American. Last year, there was a report that came out in Los Angeles that showed the rates of breast cancer in Japanese-American women, out of all ethnicities in Los Angeles County, are rising faster than any other ethnic group. I think that's pretty alarming. But in talking to other Asian women, they're all still getting that same story: that they don't have to worry because Asian women don't get breast cancer. So I have a lot more work to do. But over the past twelve years, it's been one of my major messages. It doesn't matter who you are or what you look like, what your ethnicity is, you are at risk for breast cancer. . . .

Be Your Own Advocate

It's really important that you be an advocate for yourself or find somebody who's willing to advocate for you. Unfortunately, you don't really learn this until you go through the whole experience of having cancer and having to deal with the medical community. Certainly, there are some wonderful doctors out there, but in general the medical establishment, in my opinion, is going to try to get by with as little as they possibly can. You have to demand the right treatment, you have to demand quality treatment, and you have to demand that they listen to you. Sometimes they don't like it when you do that, but you have to do it.

My name is Susan. I was diagnosed with breast cancer in 1991. I had a recurrence in 1997. And I was diagnosed with a second primary breast cancer in 2001.

And I'm still here.

Live strong.

Blogging a Battle with Cancer

Leroy Sievers

Cancer strikes victims from every walk of life. In the following selection Leroy Sievers, a highly successful television journalist, shares excerpts from his daily blog on surviving with the disease. The excerpts follow a week and a day in the life of a cancer survivor. It opens with good news from the oncologist: Sievers appears to be tumor free. By the end, however, Sievers is reflecting on the sober knowledge that very likely cancer continues to lurk somewhere in his body, waiting for the opportunity to reemerge. Rather than let this depress him, Sievers determines to enjoy whatever remains of his life to the fullest extent possible.

In May 2006, following his diagnosis, Leroy Sievers began a National Public Radio Morning Edition commentary on his fight with cancer. Sievers has been a journalist for more than twenty-five years. He worked at ABC News' Nightline for fourteen years, the last four as executive producer.

After that day, your life is never the same. "That day" is the day the doctor tells you, "You have cancer." Every one of us knows someone who's had to face that news. It's scary, it's sad. But it's still life, and it's a life worth living. "My Cancer" [the author's daily blog] is a daily account of my life and my fight with cancer.

April 30, 2007

Good News and a Trip to the Bakery The phone rang about 9 on Friday morning. At least I thought it did. I was in the shower and didn't get to it in time. There was no message on the machine. Maybe I just imagined it. I was waiting for the call from my oncologist with the results of my brain scan. But

Leroy Sievers, "My Cancer," *National Public Radio*, May 2007. Reproduced by permission of the author.

9 a.m. seemed too early for the results to be in. Did that mean good news? It was so clean it took them no time to read it? Or was it bad news, a new tumor so large it was obvious? Or was it just a wrong number?

For the previous 24 hours, I had been playing the usual games with myself, trying to get ready for bad news. This latest scan was especially important. There had been some controversy over the previous one. The initial read had been a new tumor. But after a more detailed look, my doctors said no tumor. Thursday's scan was supposed to settle the issue once and for all . . . at least for now.

Finally, about 11 a.m., my oncologist called. I have to admit, my heart started racing. He's very good; he says hello and then gives me the answer. This time, everything was clean. He said he had made sure the radiologists were extra thorough, so there would be no confusion.

I think you get a little giddy when you get good news. At least I do.

When we finally hung up, I sort of deflated, let out a long breath and just sat there for a little while. One more hurdle crossed. I know I'm not completely in the clear. I'm not cured. I'm pretty certain there's cancer hiding somewhere in my body. But so far, we haven't found it.

When I was first diagnosed a year and a half ago, my doctors said they wanted to buy me time. As much time as they could. I think they've succeeded in that. Each clean scan means a little more time free from the disease. Time I never thought I'd have. So I think I may go out and treat myself to something. I mean, it's important to celebrate good news, right? Usually with something chocolate? Of course, I say the same thing about bad news, then I need a treat to make myself feel better.

But today, that treat is going to be extra sweet. Oh yeah, my next scan is already set: June 6. Probably a full-body scan. But there's lots of time between now and then. I'm heading to the bakery.

May 1, 2007

Why Is Cancer News? I was talking with a friend of mine the other day about the upcoming documentary [on cancer being produced by the Discovery Channel]. He asked me, "Why is this news?" When I was producing *Nightline* and someone asked me that question, my response was, "It's news because I say it is." I wasn't just being sarcastic. At every media company, there are a handful of people who have the responsibility each day of deciding what stories to cover. They decide what everyone else will see or read. They decide what's news.

So why is cancer news? The obvious answer is because it affects so many people. But that's been the case for many years, and yet months have gone by with no stories about the disease. Certainly the case of Elizabeth Edwards [wife of presidential candidate John Edwards] has focused more attention on it, just as [champion cyclist] Lance Armstrong's did before.

The flip side of all that is that some outlets, having done a story or two recently, probably feel that they've done cancer, at least for now. Time to move on to something else. We in the media have a notoriously short attention span. Find a story, cover it, move on.

So I was pretty surprised when I saw the front page of the Sunday *New York Times*. There in the center of the page was a story about chemo brain. The piece focused mainly on women who have gone through chemo for breast cancer, but I think all of us who have had chemo know exactly what they're talking about. That fuzziness that can come on with the drugs. In some cases, sadly, it seems not to go away. And the story said that chemo brain is finally being looked at as something real, something that needs to be treated.

I was glad to see the story given such prominence, and I have to admit I was surprised. So often stories about cancer deal with the "latest breakthrough" or the "next breakthrough" or, of course, the "next latest breakthrough." There was one other thing that I thought was really important about the piece in the *Times*. It didn't focus on experts or trends or the latest numbers showing rates of various things over the years. No, it did something much more important. It talked about what it's like to live with cancer. It talked about the patients and what they go through. It talked about us.

May 2, 2007

A Daily Reminder That We're Not Alone I've been doing a lot of radio interviews about the Discovery Channel documentary. And almost every one of the anchors asks me the same question: "What do you get out of writing the blog?" I think many of them expect me to say that it's cathartic, that it helps me to talk about it. But that's not really the way I feel, and it's not the answer I give.

There are times when we can forget that we have cancer. Sometimes they only last for a moment, other times for hours. And I came to treasure those times. But writing the blog forces me to stop each day and think about my cancer. To think about where I am today, how I feel, what's the latest and just what's on my mind. It forces me to focus on my cancer whether I want to or not. Now, that's not a complaint at all. I actually think it's good to stop and think, to reflect on today. It's too easy sometimes to get caught up in all of the little things that make up our daily lives.

Obviously, I'm not bashful about talking about cancer. It's a little too late for that. As I continue to do this, it becomes easier. It's a conversation with friends. And all of you bring up ideas that I had never thought of.

But I do have an answer to that question, "What do you get out of writing the blog?": A daily reminder that none of us walks this road alone. What could be better than that?

May 3, 2007

The Specter of Our Own Deaths There's really only one thing that's tougher to talk about than cancer, and that's death. As we have talked about on this blog before, death is the elephant in the room. When we say we're fighting cancer, coping with it or trying to live with it, really what we're talking about is the specter of our own deaths.

Jane wrote in the other day to say how difficult it is to talk about, and she wondered if we're not in a state of denial. I don't think so. I think every cancer patient knows what this is really all about. Of course, everyone knows that they're going to die. But for most people, that's something way off in the future. When you're young, you're invincible. You think it may not happen to you, and certainly not because of all of the really stupid things we do when we're just starting our lives. As you get older, death comes for other generations—our grandparents and ultimately our parents.

And then there comes the time when it starts to sink in that it happens to us: friends, people our age. We can no longer ignore it. But I think each of us hoped that death would come for us when we're much older. We believed that we still had a lot of time.

Well, cancer changes all of that, of course. Predictions of our deaths are laid out not in decades, but in years and even months. Death is always in the room, sometimes sitting quietly in the corner, sometimes getting right in our faces. I think the biggest thing that separates us from the people who don't live in cancer world is not the pain, not the treatments, not the fear or sadness. It's that we have a pretty good idea of what's going to kill us, and a pretty good idea of when that might happen. Some of the mystery is taken away.

That doesn't mean that we should give in to hopelessness. Quite the contrary, I think it just means that for us, death is more a part of our daily lives. But as [journalist and author] Hunter Thompson said, "Buy the ticket and take the ride." The ride is no fun if there's no risk, if there's no danger— even if it's an illusion of danger. But that doesn't mean we shouldn't take our hands off the safety rail, hold them above our heads and scream like crazy. What have we got to lose?

May 4, 2007

What if I Had Never Had Cancer? I had my car in for service this morning, and I was sitting in the waiting room. The TV was on. But I wasn't paying attention until [actor] Morgan Freeman came on and started talking about colon cancer. He was urging people to have colonoscopies and said that colon cancer is one of the most treatable cancers, if caught early. Absolutely right.

And that made me think about something that I rarely consider. What if? What if I had gone for a colonoscopy as soon as I realized that it ran in my family? Instead, I waited more than five years.

If I had gone in earlier, instead of seeing the frozen face of my doctor that told me immediately that I had cancer, would he have been smiling? Would he have told me that they found some polyps, but had removed them before they could become malignant?

I usually don't dwell on the past, there's not much reason to. But what if? It's like wondering how your life would be different if you left your house five minutes earlier, or later, today. We make a million different decisions every day, some large, most small. But they all help determine the path we follow. Change one, and who knows how our lives would change? That's long been fodder for science fiction.

So I'm going to indulge myself, just this once, and stick with that question: what if? If I had never had cancer, who would I be? What would I be doing? I certainly wouldn't be writing this blog. I probably wouldn't have spent any time thinking about the things that we talk about here every day, and my life would have been poorer for that. "Who would I be?" is a little tougher to answer.

We often talk about the things we have learned from cancer, the things we have gained. It's always strange to say that there have been benefits, some positive things, but there have been. I am who I am right now, to a large degree, because of my cancer. It's been a high price to pay, no question. But I think that I am a better person than I was. My body may not be all that happy when I say that, but it's true. I am not happy that I have had to go through this, that my friends and family have had to suffer too. But I am grateful for what it has taught me. I really don't know how to reconcile all this. But now I guess I have to decide whether to leave the house now . . . or five minutes from now.

May 7, 2007

Hawaii: It's Just a Vacation, Really! I'm going on vacation. Going to Hawaii, one of my favorite places in the world. Ordinarily, when you tell people something like that, they all say how great it is. But this time, when I told my friends, there have been some awkward silences. I have to quickly say, "No, I'm not dying." I'd better explain.

When I was first diagnosed, I told my doctors I didn't want to die in a hospital, connected to machines and with tubes coming out of me. My plan was to go to Hawaii and drink mai tais until the end. I made my doctors promise to tell me when it was time for me to go to Hawaii. It may sound silly, but this was a serious conversation.

Now there was one hole in my plan that I never quite worked out. What if I timed it wrong? What if I went to Hawaii and then survived for weeks . . . or months? Then I would just become "that old drunk that sits out by the pool." I still haven't figured that part out yet.

So it came as a shock earlier this year, when my doctor suggested it was time to go. He quickly added that it was not because my death was imminent. It wasn't. But my case was going badly. The chemo had failed, the tumors had grown and spread, and we were starting to talk about getting my affairs in order, as they say. It was unlikely that I would survive past the summer, let alone to the end of the year.

He felt that at the time of that conversation, I was probably feeling as good as I was going to feel. And so it would be a good time for Hawaii. One last vacation while I could enjoy it.

Well, a lot has changed since then. Through radiation and a relatively new procedure called radio frequency ablation, we have managed to kill the tumors we knew about. My recent scans have been clean. And while I'm always quick to add that I'm not cured, that it's pretty certain the cancer is in there somewhere, right now I'm in pretty good shape. I'm in a place where I never thought I'd be.

So this is going to be a real vacation, the first one since this ordeal began. I can't wait. I do own several Hawaiian shirts. But I like to think that, as Hawaiian shirts go, they're not too bad. When I was at *Nightline*, I actually instituted Hawaiian Shirt Fridays, a step beyond Casual Fridays. That may be one reason I'm no longer there.

But I'm going over there not because it's the last trip I'm going to make. No, I'm going over there just like the thousands of tourists who go every week. To get away for a little while. And that first Mai Tai? It's going to be sweet. And, oh yeah, I am going to continue to write the blog from over there . . . but I think I'll write early in the day. Before it's mai tai time.

Organizations to Contact

The editors have compiled the following list of organizations concerned with the issues presented in this book. The descriptions are derived from materials provided by the organizations. All have publications or information available for interested readers. The list was compiled on the date of publication of the present volume; the information provided here may change. Be aware that many organizations take several weeks or longer to respond to inquiries, so allow as much time as possible.

Abramson Cancer Center
3400 Spruce Street - 2 Donner, Philadelphia, PA   19104
(215) 746-5520 • fax:(215) 349-5445
Web site: www.oncolink.com

The Abramson Cancer Center is an endowed unit of the University of Pennsylvania. It is dedicated to the eradication of cancer through research, but it also provides a great deal of support to cancer patients and their families. The center maintains a Web site, which includes a wealth of information in both English and Spanish, as well as a poetry page about cancer.

American Association for Cancer Research
615 Chestnut Street, Seventeenth Floor
Philadelphia, PA   19106
(215) 440-9300 • fax: (215) 440-7228
e-mail: aacr@aacr.org

Founded in 1907 by doctors and scientists eager to discover a cure for cancer, the American Association for Cancer Research has grown into the largest private body focused on cancer research in the world. It publishes several journals, offers workshops and conferences, and helps promote research into cancer.

American Cancer Society
1599 Clifton Road NE, Atlanta, GA   30329
(800) 228-2345
Web site: www.cancer.org

The American Cancer Society is a nationwide community-based health organization dedicated to eliminating cancer as a major health problem by prevention, treatment, and patient care through research, education, advocacy, and service. It is headquartered in Atlanta, Georgia.

American Society of Clinical Oncology (ASCO)
1900 Duke Street, Suite 200, Alexandria, VA   22314
(703) 299-0150
Web site: www.asco.org

The American Society of Clinical Oncology (ASCO) is a non-profit organization, founded in 1964. It has the overarching goals of improving cancer care and prevention and ensuring that all patients with cancer receive care of the highest quality. Nearly twenty-five thousand oncology practitioners belong to ASCO, representing all oncology disciplines (medical, radiological, and surgical) and subspecialties.

The Candlelighters Childhood Cancer Foundation (CCCF)
PO Box 498, Kensington, MD   20895
(800) 366-2223 • fax: (301) 962-3521
e-mail: staff@candlelighters.org

The Candlelighters Childhood Cancer Foundation (CCCF) is an international network that offers information and support to children with cancer and their families. Its publications include newsletters, a resource list of publications, and books and pamphlets about childhood cancer.

Centers for Disease Control and Prevention (CDC)
Division of Cancer Prevention and Control
Atlanta, GA   30341

(800) CDC-INFO • fax: (770) 488-4760
e-mail: cdcinfo@cdc.gov

The Centers for Disease Control and Prevention (CDC) is among the nation's leaders in efforts to ease the burden of cancer. Through the Division of Cancer Prevention and Control, the CDC works with national cancer organizations, state health agencies, and other key groups to develop, implement, and promote effective strategies for preventing and controlling cancer.

Corporate Angel Network
Westchester County Airport, White Plains, NY   10604
(914) 328-1313 • fax: (914) 328-3938
e-mail: info@corpangelnetwork.org

The Corporate Angel Network is a charitable organization in the United States whose sole mission is to ease the emotional stress, physical discomfort, and financial burden of travel for cancer patients by arranging free flights to treatment centers. It makes use of donations of empty seats on corporate aircraft flying on routine business.

Foundation for Advancement in Cancer Therapy (FACT)
PO Box 1242, Old Chelsea Station, New York, NY   10113
(212) 741-2790

The Foundation for Advancement in Cancer Therapy (FACT) distributes information about alternative treatments for cancer that it considers safe and nontoxic. It believes that tumors are symptoms of a gradual breakdown in the balance of body chemistry and that treatments should focus on correcting this imbalance and building up the body's resistance to cancer rather than on destroying the tumors themselves. The foundation publishes the bimonthly newsletter *Cancer Forum*, a book list, and pamphlets such as What Is *F.A.C.T.?*

Lance Armstrong Foundation
PO Box 161150, Austin, TX   78716

(512) 236-8820
e-mail: livestrongchallenge@laf.org

The Lance Armstrong Foundation was created by champion cyclist Lance Armstrong, who was diagnosed with testicular cancer in the midst of a string of Tour de France championships. Armstrong underwent successful treatment and went on to win several more championships. The Lance Armstrong Foundation gives hope and encouragement to cancer survivors. Its Web site includes the inspiring story of its founder and many other cancer survivors.

Mayo Clinic
200 First Street SW, Rochester, MN   55905
(507) 284-2511 • fax: (507) 284-0161
Web site: www. mayoclinic.org

The famed Mayo Clinic, based in Rochester, Minnesota, is a not-for-profit medical center that diagnoses and treats complex medical problems in every specialty, including a wide variety of cancers. The Mayo Clinic maintains a great Web site for the public with more than six hundred articles and entries on virtually every type of cancer.

National Cancer Institute (NCI)
6116 Executive Boulevard, Bethesda, MD   20892
(800) 422-6237
Web site: www.cancer.gov

The National Cancer Institute (NCI), established under the National Cancer Institute Act of 1937, is the federal government's principal agency for cancer research and training. It expanded in 1971 following President Richard Nixon's declaration of a national "war on cancer." Today it supports a broad range of cancer research and treatment programs.

National Foundation for Cancer Research (NFCR)
4600 East West Highway, Suite 525, Bethesda, MD   20814

(800) 321-2873
e-mail: info@nfcr.org

The National Foundation for Cancer Research (NFCR) was founded in 1973 to support cancer research and public education about prevention, early diagnosis, treatment, and ultimately, a cure for cancer. NFCR promotes and facilitates collaboration among scientists to accelerate the pace of productive cancer research.

Oncology Nursing Society (ONS)
125 Enterprise Drive, Pittsburgh, PA   15275
(866) 257-4667 • fax: (877) 369-5497
e-mail: customer.service@ons.org

The Oncology Nursing Society (ONS) is a professional organization of more than thirty-three thousand registered nurses and other health-care providers dedicated to excellence in patient care, education, research, and administration in oncology nursing. Its award-winning Web site provides information on a wide range of possible symptoms of cancer. It also has an "ask a nurse" feature.

Susan G. Komen for the Cure
5005 LBJ Freeway, Suite 250, Dallas, TX   75244
(800) 462-9273 • fax: (972) 855-1605
Web site: cms.komen.org

Susan G. Komen for the Cure was launched in 1982 by the sister of a breast cancer victim whose name the organization bears. Today it claims to be the world's largest grassroots network of breast cancer survivors and activists. In its effort to cure breast cancer at every stage, the organization has invested $1 billion in research, education, and health services.

Bibliography

Books

American Cancer Society
Quick Facts Lung Cancer: What You Need to Know—Now. Atlanta: American Cancer Society, 2007.

American Urological Association
Prostate Cancer Awareness for Men. Baltimore: American Urological Association, 2000.

Greg Anderson
Cancer: 50 Essential Things to Do. New York: Penguin, 1999.

Sudipta Bardhan-Quallen
Chemotherapy. Farmington Hills, MI: Lucent, 2003.

Debbie Bookchin and Jim Schumacher
The Virus and the Vaccine: The True Story of a Cancer-Causing Monkey Virus, Contaminated Polio Vaccine, and the Millions of Americans Exposed. New York: St. Martin's, 2004.

Centers for Disease Control and Prevention
Prostate Cancer: Can We Reduce Deaths and Preserve Quality of Life? At-a-Glance 1999. Atlanta: Centers for Disease Control and Prevention, 1999.

Helen S. L. Chan
Understanding Cancer Therapies. Jackson: University Press of Mississippi, 2007.

Kristine Conner and Lauren Langford
Ovarian Cancer: Your Guide to Taking Control. Cambridge, MA: O'Reilly Media, 2003.

Elizabeth Edwards *Saving Graces: Finding Solace and Strength from Friends and Strangers.* Waterville, ME: Thorndike, 2007.

Federal Trade Commission *Up in Smoke: The Truth About Tar and Nicotine Ratings.* Washington, DC: Federal Trade Commission, Bureau of Consumer Protection, Office of Consumer and Business Education, 2000.

Wendy S. Harpham *When a Parent Has Cancer: A Guide to Caring for Your Children.* New York: HarperCollins, 1997.

Bernadine Healy *Living Time: Faith and Facts to Transform Your Cancer Journey.* New York: Bantam, 2007.

Carolyn M. Kaelin *The Breast Cancer Survivor's Fitness Plan: Reclaim Health, Regain Strength, Live Longer.* New York: McGraw-Hill, 2007.

David G. Nathan *The Cancer Treatment Revolution: How Smart Drugs and Other New Therapies Are Renewing Our Hope and Changing the Face of Medicine.* Hoboken, NJ: Wiley, 2007.

Jenny Penson and Ronald Fisher *Palliative Care for People with Cancer,* 3rd ed. London, UK: Hodder Education, 2002.

Lisa Shaw-Brawley *Only When I Sleep: My Family's Journey Through Cancer.* Deerfield Beach, FL: HCI, 2000.

Marc Silver — *Breast Cancer Husband: How to Help Your Wife (and Yourself) During Diagnosis, Treatment and Beyond.* Emmaus, PA: Rodale, 2004.

U.S. Department of Health and Human Services, Public Health Service, National Institutes of Health, National Cancer Institute — *Risks Associated with Smoking Cigarettes with Low Machine-Measured Yields of Tar and Nicotine.* Bethesda, MD: National Institutes of Health, 2001.

U.S. Surgeon General — *Health Consequences of Involuntary Exposure to Tobacco Smoke: A Report of the Surgeon General.* Atlanta: Centers for Disease Control and Prevention, 2006.

Ben Williams — *Surviving Terminal Cancer: Clinical Trials, Drug Cocktails, and Other Treatments Your Oncologist Won't Tell You About.* Minneapolis, MN: Fairview, 2002.

Periodicals

M. Natalie Achong — "What Women Need to Know About HPV and Cervical Cancer," *Ebony,* July 2007.

C.B. Ambrosone — "Impact of Genetics on the Relationship Between Smoking and Breast Cancer Risk," *Journal of Women's Cancer,* no. 3, 2001.

Associated Press   "No Cancer Shield Found in Fruit and Vegetable Diet," *New York Times*, July 17, 2007.

Christen Brownlee   "Fat Could Hinder Body's Fight Against Disease," *Science News*, October 28, 2006,

Penny Cottee   "Suffering in Silence?" *People Management*, October 2006.

Peter Duesberg   "Chromosomal Chaos and Cancer," *Scientific American*, May 2007.

Denise Grady   "Researchers Find Distinctive Patterns of Cancer in 5 Groups of Asian-Americans," *New York Times*, July 11, 2007.

Wendy S. Harpham   "Note to My Nurse: View from the Other Side of the Stethoscope," *Oncology Times*, February 25, 2007.

Harvard Men's Health Watch   "Lifestyle Therapy for Prostate Cancer: Does It Work?" July 2007.

Harvard Women's Health Watch   "Drop in Breast Cancer May Reflect Decline in Hormone Use," July 2007.

Judith Hooper   "Cancer's New Rules," *Prevention*, November 2005.

Shia Kapos   "Cancer vs. Career: How Couples Cope," *Crain's Chicago Business*, April 9, 2007.

Ulrike Peters et al.	"Selenium and Risk of Prostate Cancer: A Nested Case-Control *Study*," *American Journal of Clinical Nutrition*, January 2007.
Andrew Pollack	"Shark Cartilage, Not a Cancer Therapy," *New York Times*, June 3, 2007.
Reuters	"Lung Cancer Tied to Family Risk of Other Cancers," May 11, 2007.
John D. Schell	"Tungsten Alloy and Cancer in Rats: Link to Childhood Leukemia?" *Environmental Health Perspectives*, December 2005.
Jerry W. Shay	"Telomerase in Cancer: Diagnostic, Prognostic and Therapeutic Implications," *Cancer Journal of Scientific American*, April 1998.
Michael J. Thun	"Editorial: More Misleading Science from the Tobacco Industry," *British Medical Journal*, July 30, 2003.
Tufts University Health & Nutrition Letter	"Carving Out Connections Between Meats and Breast Cancer Risk," July 2007.

Internet Sources

American Cancer Society, "What Are the Risk Factors for Breast Cancer?" September 18, 2006. www.cancer.org.

Will Dunham, "Lots of Fruit, Vegetables Don't Stop Breast Cancer," Reuters, July 17, 2007. www.sciam.com/article.cfm?alias=lots-of-fruit-vegetables.

Nancy Gay, "Preventing Colon Cancer," News 13, July 24, 2007. www.cfnews13.com/Health/YourHealth/2007/7/23/preventing-colon-cancer.html.

Greg Lester, "Gene Variations Directly Link Inflammation to an Increased Risk for Lung Cancer," American Association for Cancer Research, July 3, 2007. www.eurekalert.org/pub-releases/2007-07/aafc-gvd070207.php.

Medical News Today, "Racial Differences in Severity of Breast Cancer Presentation Confirmed," July 18, 2007. www.medicalnewstoday.com/articles/77054.php.

Robert Preidt, "Supplements Don't Cut Lung Cancer Risk: Study," HealthDay, May 21, 2007. www.healthday.com/Article.asp?AID=604712.

Melissa Conrad Stoppler, "Lung Cancer," MedicineNet. March 24, 2005.www.medicinenet.com/lung-cancer/article.htm.

Anne Trafton, "MIT IDs Role of Key Protein in Tumor Growth," MIT News, March 15, 2007. http://web.mit.edu/newsoffice/2007/tumorigenesis.html.

Index